Presented to:

_____

From:

_____

Date:

_____

Real Answers for the
Tough Questions Teens Ask

by Jim Burns

HONOR **HB** BOOKS

Inspiration and Motivation for the Seasons of Life

COOK COMMUNICATIONS MINISTRIES
Colorado Springs, Colorado • Paris, Ontario
KINGSWAY COMMUNICATIONS LTD
Eastbourne, England

Honor Books® is an imprint of
Cook Communications Ministries, Colorado Springs, Colorado 80918
Cook Communications, Paris, Ontario
Kingsway Communications Ltd, Eastbourne, England

Truth Unplugged–Strait Talk for Teens About Life: Real Answers for the Tough Questions
Copyright © 2005 by Jim Burns

First printing, 2005
Printed in the United States of America
Printing/Year
11 10 9 8 7 6 5 4 / 05 06 07 08 09

ISBN 1-56292-218-1

Introduction

Where can you go for answers to the tough issues you face? *Truth Unplugged—Straight Talk for Teens* about Life gives you facts and solid advice about the experiences that confront you in the hall, on the way to class, in the parking lot after school, or at a friend's house—things such as why you should not smoke, how to relate to the opposite sex, how to cope with harassment from a bully, or even what to do when a friend gets really low and talks about dying.

These important answers come straight from Jim Burns, an expert who has been giving sound, Godly wisdom to teens for years. The real answers for the tough questions asked and answered in the following pages will help you make good decisions and defend those decisions under pressure while growing closer to God.

A MOUNTAIN OF CONFIDENCE

How do I overcome anxieties and fears? When I know God has given me something to say, I get really nervous. I almost feel like I'm going to pass out.

Face your fears by working through them. The more you speak about God and say what He wants you to say, the less nervous and anxious you will be.

I'd also encourage you to talk to your youth worker or pastor at church. They know you and your personality traits and can give you better advice on how to confidently say what God wants you to say. Seek the advice and accountability of people who know you, support you, and want to see you speak with integrity and pure motives.

Another good way to gain confidence is to sign up for a speech class, the debate team, or the drama club. The teachers and directors in those areas will give you some good tips for public speaking, and you can take those skills into any social situation, even one-on-one. Though you probably won't be talking about God or your faith in these situations, you'll likely grow more confident to talk about anything.

Although I've never passed out when talking about God, there are times when I feel anxiety about what I feel I'm supposed to say.

What do I do in times such as these? Take a deep breath, offer a prayer, and go for it. And that's my encouragement to you too.

Confidence is a mountain of repeated successful experiences created over time.

LET THE WORDS OF MY MOUTH AND THE MEDITATION OF MY HEART BE ACCEPTABLE IN YOUR SIGHT, O LORD, MY ROCK AND MY REDEEMER.

PSALM 19:14 NASB

YOU WIN

I have been aware of my same-sex attractions since the age of sixteen. I had one dating relationship towards the end of high school and a brief relationship after the first year of college. From the onset, however, I have always believed the Bible's position on homosexuality as being a sin and have wanted to change. I have abstained from pursuing same-sex relationships for the past four years and have been part of a church and the campus fellowship at my church. Should I take a break from school and move to a place where Christ-centered counseling is available?

I have been interested in entering a counseling program to seek healing in my sexual identity. Unfortunately, there are no counselors that I, or my pastor, know of in the area. The closest one is about an hour away, and I don't have a car.

. . . I feel strongly that I should do something formal and constructive to address these same-sex desires. I have become very depressed, afraid that people will find out my "secret" and that the campus fellowship

(in which I have done a lot of serving) will be discredited if people start thinking that one of its most visible members is gay. In any case, I don't feel comfortable talking to my friends about it, but I need to do something.

It sounds like you have a good handle on your same-sex attractions. The key for long-term change is going to be counseling and support from someone who understands where you are coming from, and your unique needs and circumstances.

First, the counseling issue. It really is imperative that you find some Christ-centered counseling options. Since you haven't found anyone in your area, this could present a problem. You may want to call Exodus International and see if they know about someone in your area. See below for a listing of contact information for them and some other organizations that might be able to help you with locating someone in your area.

You may need to pursue going to the counselor who is an hour away. It might be easier to find a car than to find another option.

As for the ministry and school issue, the truth is that having same-sex attractions is not a sin, but acting on them is. From what you've written, you aren't in an area of sin yet. If you are going to continue in ministry, consider the following:

1. You will need to find an accountability partner whom you can be honest with.

2. You will need to find some counseling options in order to seek healing and wholeness in this area.

3. If you are really struggling, you may need to take a break from ministry in order to focus more on your own personal healing than the healing and wholeness of others.

Here are a few contacts for you.

- Exodus International 1-888-264-0877 or 206-7784-7799 or www.exodus.to
- Breaking New Ground (Portland Fellowship) www.portlandfellowship.com
- Homosexuals Anonymous 215-376-1146
- Courage/St. John the Baptist Church and Friary 212-421-0426
- NARTH (National Association of Research and Treatment of Homosexuality) 818-789-4440
- Desert Stream Ministries 714-779-6899 or www.desertstream.org

TO THEM GOD CHOSE TO MAKE KNOWN HOW GREAT AMONG THE GENTILES ARE THE RICHES OF THE GLORY OF THIS MYSTERY, WHICH IS CHRIST IN YOU, THE HOPE OF GLORY.

COLOSSIANS 1:27
NRSV

You can overcome any obstacle in your life when you're pursuing a constant relationship with God.

REAL LOVE

What is the difference between love and infatuation?

In my opinion, much of what people call "love" is just "infatuation." Infatuation has a lot to do with physical attraction and the "warm fuzzies" of a person's thought life (like "Oh, I'm SO in love . . . with that person I just met."). While a lot of the feelings of infatuation are the same as they are in real love, love is MORE than a feeling. Here are some major differences:

- Real love involves commitment to the other person; infatuation doesn't.

- Real love is more about how I can show I care for the other person; infatuation is more about how the other person makes ME feel.

- Real love is based on really knowing the other person; infatuation focuses on the physical qualities and impressions about the other person.

- Real love lasts through disagreements and trials; disagreements and trials often "burst the bubble" of infatuation.

- Real love stands the test of time; infatuation doesn't last.

Having said all of this, I want you to be aware that infatuation is normal. It is often the introduction to real love—the first stage of a romantic relationship. For instance, a guy is attracted to a girl (or vice versa). They meet. They like each other (infatuation). They begin to develop a relationship. The relationship either blossoms (into love), stagnates (remains infatuation for a while), or dies (the bubble bursts!).

A great Biblical tool to help determine love from infatuation is found in 1 Corinthians 13. In this chapter, Paul writes about the characteristics of real love. I suggest that you take a look!

Real love stands the test of time.

**NOW ABIDE FAITH, HOPE, LOVE,
THESE THREE; BUT THE GREATEST
OF THESE IS LOVE.**

1 CORINTHIANS 13:13 NKJV

OPEN UP

What can I do to help my parents realize that it is important to me for them to know more about what it feels like to be an adopted kid? I'm adopted, and I don't think my parents have any idea of how adoption affects me. I don't feel like I can really talk to them about it. I love my parents, and I know they care about me.

You are dealing with a very important issue. As a parent who has an adopted daughter, I feel it's important to try really hard to understand what adoption means to an adopted child. And I would be surprised if your parents didn't feel the same way. Check in with them again to make sure there isn't just a communication problem.

Sometimes parents have a tough time expressing their feelings, or your parents might feel a bit afraid that you will reject them. Reassure them of your love. They may not be your birth parents, but since they raised you, they are your parents, and I'm sure you love them dearly.

Each adoption is different and special. In any family, it's important to find the right time to talk about your feelings and frustrations, your dreams and desires. Tell your parents how you feel, and tell them what you wish you could receive from them as you reassure them of their place in your life. I'd even recommend letting your parents read your question and my answer. It may help all three of you talk more openly about your adoption. You also may want to suggest that the three of you read something together. One book I'd recommend is *Loved by Choice* by Susan Horner and Kelly Fordyce Martindale (Baker). The book is really a celebration of adoption, and it comes with a list of resources that could provide further reading for you and/or your parents. Maybe you could read a chapter or a part of a chapter after dinner each night.

I encourage you to be gentle when talking with them about reading a book about adoption. Try hard not to be critical or make them think they aren't doing enough to understand your feelings. Just present it as a way to better understand what adoption means to the whole family. Reading something together also may help each of you talk more easily about your feelings and thoughts on adoption. One of the greatest days of my life was the day we brought my daughter home. A social worker placed this precious girl in my arms, and with tears in my eyes, I thanked God for giving me such a special gift. Today my daughter is a teenager, and hardly a day goes by that I do not thank God for bringing her into my life.

> **YOU HAVE RECEIVED A SPIRIT OF ADOPTION AS SONS BY WHICH WE CRY OUT, "ABBA! FATHER!"**
>
> **ROMANS 8:15 NASB**

Your parents probably feel the same way about you. As someone who is adopted, you might feel the intensity of abandonment at certain milestones in your life, like your birthdays and graduation. At these times, remember that you are a special gift from God given to your parents by a birth mom. God, your birth mom, and your parents brought you to the place you are today. Learn all you can about your special place in life; try hard to express your feelings to your parents; and thank God for the way He passionately cares for you.

Communication begins with an open heart and mind, speaking from a point of truth and listening with a willingness to consider a fresh new perspective.

CELEBRATE YOUR PERSONALITY

How can I be more outgoing? I'm kind of introverted, and I get intimidated easily. When I'm around some people, I just don't say anything. When I do speak, I feel like it comes out jumbled up and dumb. Every time I am myself, I feel like people are looking at me strangely. I feel like people don't know the real me. I talk a lot at home, but in church I'm not as open. I just wish I could act the same with everyone. When I see outgoing people, I wish I could be outgoing too.

You are in the process of growing toward maturity. Most people feel the way you do at some time. I'm outgoing, and just yesterday, I was with a group of people who totally intimidated me. I felt like my words were "jumbled up" and I felt "dumb" too. It's true we're more comfortable at home and in any environment where we feel at ease. There are certain places where an introvert feels more comfortable and certain places where an extrovert is more at ease. Let me tell you why I like introverts. They are usually much better listeners than extroverts, and listening is the language of love. They are often more sensitive to others' needs. They may not talk as much as extroverts, but when they do, they often have something very important to say. They think before they speak; I speak and think at the same time, and it sometimes doesn't make sense. Introverts can go to a social gathering or church youth group and have a very good and meaningful conversation with one person. In the same situation, we extroverts will far too often just have a shallow conversation with everyone.

I hope you'll learn to celebrate your personality. Extroverts may seem to have the handle on words and social settings, but I think a secure introvert who loves God and has a proper self-image is the strongest influence in the world. Instead of worrying too much about being an introvert, acknowledge God's creation of your life and even His part in creating your personality.

Celebrate being you.

YOU CREATED MY INMOST BEING; YOU KNIT ME TOGETHER IN MY MOTHER'S WOMB. I PRAISE YOU BECAUSE I AM FEARFULLY AND WONDERFULLY MADE; YOUR WORKS ARE WONDERFUL, I KNOW THAT FULL WELL.

PSALM 139:13-14

IT'S YOUR CHOICE

I was just thinking about Genesis and the Garden of Eden; why did God tell Adam and Eve not to eat the forbidden fruit? My question is why did God put the tree with the forbidden fruit in there? And why didn't God kick out Satan from the Garden of Eden, or why didn't He have the angels keep him out?

I don't think anyone can state with certainty why God did what He did in the early acts of the human drama. For all we can know about God, we won't know everything about Him—certainly not in this life. In many ways, God is beyond our own comprehension.

God, through the prophet Isaiah said this about himself: "For my thoughts are not your thoughts, neither are your ways my ways," declares the LORD. "As the heavens are higher than the earth, so are my ways higher than your ways and my thoughts than your thoughts" (Isaiah 55:8-9).

With that understanding, let me give you some of MY thoughts. I hope that you will find them helpful!

• God didn't create people as robots. Part of what makes us "persons" is that God has given us freedom of choice. If He had simply made us always choose what He wanted us to do, I think it might take away from the significance of our choices to love, obey, and follow Him.

• I know in my life, my own sin ruined me and separated me from God. I know it was costly for God to offer me the forgiveness I need and only He could provide. It cost Him the death of his only Son, Jesus. And now, because I know His love and forgiveness in my own life, I love Him and literally owe my life (and eternal life) to Him. I'm not sure I would have known the power of His love in such a way if Adam and Eve had not introduced sin (through Satan's deceptions) to our human family.

CHOOSE TODAY WHOM YOU WILL SERVE.

JOSHUA 24:15
NLT

• God's perfection, holiness, and glory shine all the brighter in contrast to the dark background of sin and evil.

God gave you a soul so that you could choose freely to serve Him.

IMMEDIATE AUDIENCE

Should I continue to pursue my desire to pray at school or leave it alone?

At my school, teachers and administrators are not allowed to pray aloud. Recently, I asked for permission to say a prayer before a ball game, but administrators told me this also would be against the law. One of my teachers says this isn't true. I feel like God is telling me to do this.

You are bringing up one of the most controversial issues of this generation. There have been thousands of debates and arguments over prayer in schools. There are schools, especially in the South, where prayer opens every game. However, because of Supreme Court rulings, official prayers before a school-sponsored game are not allowed. Moments of silence are allowed, but no one—adults or students—may pray aloud.

What's interesting about this ruling is that the same Supreme Court has allowed student-lead Bible clubs to meet on campus where students are free to pray. This is called the "Equal Access Act." It is perfectly legal for you and your friends to form a club and then pray on your school campus. For more information on how the "Equal

Access Act" applies to your school, go online to gocampus.org/alliance/launch/launch3-17.html.

As for your question to pursue it or leave it alone, you'll have to make that decision. I doubt your administration will allow you to pray aloud . God may be leading you to write your representatives in Washington and ask them to consider legislation to change the law. Many Christians are becoming more and more active in what they call "public policy," and I think that is a good thing. Sometimes God plants a dream in our heart to help work toward change. But for now, don't stop praying for your school—and do it while at school. No one can stop you from walking down the hall and silently praying for teachers and students. No one can stop you from bowing to say a prayer of thanks over a meal.

> **THE PRAYER OF A PERSON LIVING RIGHT WITH GOD IS SOME-THING POWERFUL TO BE RECKONED WITH.**
>
> **JAMES 5:16 MSG**

Remember, prayer is really about talking directly to God, expressing your thanks, showing your love for Him, asking for His help and guidance, and asking Him to reveal himself to those who need Him. So, do keep praying at school—even if public prayer remains forbidden.

A silent prayer gains immediate audience with the Highest Authority.

ISSUES OF LIFE

Do you know of any good Christian RPGs? I enjoy role-playing games, but I don't care for the mainstream RPGs like Dungeons and Dragons, Rifts, and Vampire. I have been able to find a few good alternative secular RPGs, but have yet to find a good Christian one.

You are not alone in your quest for Christ-honoring, role-playing games. In fact, a group of Christian game enthusiasts decided to take their interest online, and they founded the Christian Gamers Guild (CGG) in 1996. CGG was formerly known as the Christian Role-Playing Gamers Association. Though the name was changed to include all types of gamers, CGG continues to focus on RPGs. They host a newsgroup on Yahoo! and publish an e-zine complete with reviews on Christian RPGs. Their website can be found at geocities.com/christian_gamers_guild/.

There aren't a ton of Christian RPGs out there, and CGG hopes to change that. Its goals include involvement in game design, game advocacy from a Christian perspective, and ministry at game conventions.

It doesn't sound like you need this warning, but many readers may need to be reminded that RPGs can be very dangerous. As Christ followers, we must make sure we do not put negative or occult-type thoughts into our minds.

I'd like to tell you about Steve, a Christian guy who got into RPGs when he was fourteen. Steve found a Web site with lots of RPGs and joined in a few of the games. Soon, he became hooked. He sensed God was telling him that some of the games were unhealthy for his spiritual walk, but he ignored the feeling. He figured he was okay because he was still going to church.

Within a year-and-a-half, Steve found himself addicted to very intense and anti-Christian games. The addiction then moved into other areas of his life—he started looking at pornography every day.

KEEP YOUR HEART WITH ALL DILIGENCE, FOR OUT OF IT SPRING THE ISSUES OF LIFE.

PROVERBS 4:23

NKJV

Steve left the church, his friends, his faith. His grades dropped, and he was violating his value system in every way. Finally, Steve realized he was addicted.

Thankfully, there is a positive ending to Steve's story. He turned to God for help and went to his youth pastor for counseling. After some very intense months of healing, Steve is now living in freedom from the addiction. However, the vivid images are embedded in his mind, and he still lives with the consequences of addiction. Steve must keep a safe distance from anything that could come close to pulling him toward RPGs or pornography.

I really do hope that Christian gamers will soon have some creative and safe alternatives. Who knows, maybe God will use you to create some! (See Romans 12:2 and Philippians 4:8-9.) But for the sake of so many who are getting fooled into some very negative stuff, I felt I needed to expand on your question.

The path you think on is usually the path you choose to travel the most.

RIGHT MOTIVES

What does the Bible have to say about being a vegetarian? Is it okay to be one, or does it go against something God has said?

You can be a vegetarian, or you can eat meat. The Bible does not speak for it or against it. In the Bible, Daniel chose to eat vegetables instead of the food from the king's table. After ten days, he was very healthy. You can find this story in Daniel 1:8-16.

I would encourage you to check with your family doctor, a dietician, or a nutritionist before making any radical changes in your diet. If you choose to become a vegetarian, you need to do it right. That means making sure you have a healthy diet that includes getting the right amount of protein through some sort of meat substitute.

Here are two questions for you:

1. What are your motives? If you choose to be a vegetarian and it is for the right reasons, then you will have pure motives. You won't be doing it to be accepted by a friend or to go against your parents. You will make the decision with integrity.

2. Do you believe God is leading you toward being a vegetarian? If God cares about everything involved in our lives, and He does, then He surely cares about our eating decisions. (See Matthew 6:25-

33.) Seek His leadership and His guidance. Even our eating habits should bring us closer to God—if we make these decisions with the right motives and with the ultimate purpose of bringing Him glory in all we do.

A generous heart produces right motives and a clean conscience.

MIXED MOTIVES TWIST LIFE INTO TANGLES; PURE MOTIVES TAKE YOU STRAIGHT DOWN THE ROAD.

PROVERBS 21:8 MSG

OUR THOUGHTS

How do I stop? I occasionally venture into a pornographic site, and I know it's wrong. But I can't seem to break the habit. Help!

Thanks for your honesty. Pornography is an especially tough issue. The great news is that God is the God of forgiveness and restoration. No matter where you are, what you've done, or what you're trapped in—God can and will forgive, heal, and restore.

The first step is admitting that there is a problem and that it's wrong—which you have, and that's great. Half the battle is won right there. As for the future, change begins with a decision to change and then is followed through with whatever measures it takes to live out that commitment. It sounds like you're wanting to change, and that's the first step. Now begins the tough road of daily decisions that help you live out that commitment.

Here are a few decisions you may need to make:

• You may need to change your Internet software to a filtered provider, one that won't allow you to get to the Web site, even if you wanted to.

• You may need to change your Web habits, by moving the computer to a more public place in the house, if you're living with some other people.

• Gather people around you who can keep you accountable. You need to have people in your life with whom you can share your struggle—people who will ask you the tough questions in life like,

"When was the last time that you went to that site?" These are people whom you trust and know. They are transparent with you and love you unconditionally—no strings attached!

• You may have heard the saying, "garbage in, garbage out." Well, it applies here. Not only do you need to not put garbage in, you need to feed your mind with things that will purify your mind and heart. Evaluate what you read, listen to, and watch. What are the messages that you are allowing into your mind and heart? Read the Scriptures and other Christian reading.

> **ABOVE ALL ELSE, GUARD YOUR HEART, FOR IT IS THE WELL-SPRING OF LIFE.**
>
> **PROVERBS 4:23**

• Listen to music that edifies Christ. Start "reformatting" your heart and mind by the things that you allow into them.

• Check out Proverbs 4:23 and claim it as your own.

Remember, overcoming an addiction isn't easy. There are no quick fixes. It takes time, effort, and commitment. There may still be times that you fall and stumble, but God is right there. Lean on Him. Rely on the Spirit to help you get through this. Pray often. God will see you through this. You probably didn't get into this overnight, and there won't be an overnight cure. God is in the business of healing and freedom. He's done it before; He'll do it in your life as well!

Your eyes, ears, and mouth are gateways to your soul. Stand guard.

A PLACE TO CALL HOME

What do you think I need to do? About a year ago something really horrible happened at my old church, so I decided to quit going there. I've wanted to get back into the swing of things and find the closeness that comes only from a church family. The problem is, I've visited ten churches, but I still can't find a "home." I don't feel like I belong anywhere. This is starting to really bug me because I don't feel God's presence anymore, and nothing I do seems to help me get close to Him again.

I am so impressed by your desire to find a church you can commit yourself to. And being committed to a church is very important. In fact, Christ calls the Church His bride, so He obviously places a very high value on the Church. (See 2 Corinthians 11:2 and Ephesians 5:23-32.) Again, I want to commend you for your desire to be fully committed to a body of believers.

I have no idea what horrible thing happened at your previous church, so it's impossible for me to know how severe the problem was. But a lot can change in a year. Would it make sense to at least visit your old church again, just to see if things are any better? I realize it may not be easy to go back. You may even have to work hard at forgiving those who may have been responsible for whatever happened. But if it seems appropriate to do so, maybe you can return.

If going back to your previous church is simply impossible, then I must encourage you to continue your search. I also encourage you to give each church you visit a fair chance. Experts tell us it often takes a couple of years to feel at home and completely comfortable in a new congregation.

> **UNDER HIS DIRECTION, THE WHOLE BODY IS FITTED TOGETHER PERFECTLY. AS EACH PART DOES ITS OWN SPECIAL WORK, IT HELPS THE OTHER PARTS GROW, SO THAT THE WHOLE BODY IS HEALTHY AND GROWING AND FULL OF LOVE.**
>
> EPHESIANS 4:16 NLT

Here are four things for you to think about as you look for a church:

• No church is perfect, and no church will be exactly like your old one. I'd suggest you write a list of the most important things you are looking for in a church home. Be careful, though. Don't try to find the perfect church. There isn't one this side of Heaven.

• Seek the advice of your Christian friends. Sometimes people who know you well will have a good idea of the kind of church you might need and want. Listen to their advice. Are you involved in a Christian club at school? Then talk to your club leader. Also, you haven't said anything about your family. I hope you're working through this with them. If your parents are Christians, you need their support and their guidance in this matter. And if at all possible, you should try to find a church together.

• Pray for God's direction and discernment. He definitely wants you to regularly worship Him within a community of believers. So ask Him to guide you in your search.

• Be sure you're trying to build your own relationship with God. You say you're not feeling close to God right now. Even if the feeling isn't there, don't let yourself drift from personal Bible study and prayer. Keep talking honestly and openly to God and allow Him to speak to you through His Word. Read passages that bring you hope and comfort. Psalms is a great place to start. Also, find a strong Christian friend you can confide in. Pray with this friend and seek his or her counsel when you're struggling with your faith.

Let me give you one more piece of advice about church—actually, it's not original. The philosopher Søren Kierkegaard said that when you go to church you should never ask, "How was it?" But rather, when you finish with the service, you should ask, "How did I do?" In other words, as we attend church, we need to be reminded that we are to actively participate in the service and not merely be spectators. With that in mind, I hope you find a church soon that you can call home.

Unconditional love brings all the comforts of home.

BRILLIANT

Am I supposed to be a goody-two-shoes? I'm responsible, dependable, friendly, and mature, but I'm really boring. I don't believe people at school think I'm a loser; I'm just Susan, the goody-goody, Christian, nice girl.

Actually, you sound wonderful! Oh, that there were more people like you in the world! Yet, I can see where you're coming from; nobody wants to be boring. I think it's a matter of how you define boring. In my opinion, words like responsible, dependable, friendly, and Christian are anything but boring.

You remind me of Kendra, a student who was in a youth group I once led. While a youth leader isn't supposed to have favorites, I must admit Kendra was and always will be special to me. She was responsible, dependable, friendly, and a deeply committed Christian. Sound familiar? She was a leader in my youth group and had lots of friends and everybody's respect. She also sat at home during her senior prom because "everybody was asked" but her. I still remember the long and depressing talk we had about why she didn't get asked. Frankly, my youth staff and I couldn't figure it out. In our opinion, she would have been the ideal prom date. Even though I told her my opinion, it didn't help much because she was still sitting at home on that big night.

After her high school graduation, Kendra went off to a Christian college where she was very popular but still didn't date much. Like you, she would have described herself as boring, but I don't think anyone else would have described her that way. The decisions she kept making about her spiritual life and lifestyle were truly inspirational and exciting. At her university graduation, she was voted Most Inspirational Woman and Student of the Year.

Then on a summer mission trip, she met Mark, and they fell in love. During some premarital counseling I did with them, I asked Mark, "What attracted you to Kendra?" His reply was enlightening, "I have never met a more incredible and exciting person. Her depth of faith, dependability, responsibility, and overall friendliness is more than I ever dreamed of in a woman.

> **YOU ARE THE LIGHT OF THE WORLD. A CITY BUILT ON A HILL CANNOT BE HID.**
>
> MATTHEW 5:14 NRSV

She brings so very much to this relationship and so little negative baggage. She is such a loving and faithful person, and I daily see Christ in her life."

As he spoke such loving and passionate words, I felt tears fill my eyes. Kendra's faithfulness and devotion were now paying off in a wonderful relationship. Today Kendra is a most incredible wife, mother, and leader in her church. She is a "Proverbs 31" woman. (Look up this passage if you're not familiar with it.) Today, I don't believe she sees herself as boring, and I don't think she's worrying anymore about not being asked to the prom.

Here is my encouragement to you: Stay true to your values. Continue working on your faithfulness, and the result will be a life that's anything but boring.

You are a brilliant wonder in the eyes of your Creator.

KEEPING THE PEACE

If you have a hard time getting along with your parents and are rude to them, does that mean you're not a Christian? I'm a strong Christian, and I'm really into proving my faith is correct. I have memorized a lot of Bible scriptures too. I do have one really big problem though. I can't get along with my parents. We argue constantly. Sometimes I think they don't love me, and I wonder if they care more about my excelling younger sister. They told me I don't listen to the Bible, that I pretend to be a Christian, but I'm really not one because I fight with them. Is that true?

Arguing with your parents has little to do with whether or not you're a Christian. Romans 10:9-10 says, "If you confess with your mouth, 'Jesus is Lord,' and believe in your heart that God raised him from the dead, you will be saved. For it is with your heart that you believe and are justified, and it is with your mouth that you confess and are saved." If you have sincerely asked Jesus Christ to forgive your sins and have invited Him to be in your life, then you are a Christian. Now that we've settled that, let's take a look at your relationship with your parents.

It's very normal to have arguments with your mom and dad. As you move from dependence on them toward independence, you, like most teenagers, will have some bumpy times with your parents. It comes along with the territory of the teenage years. No doubt your parents could use some work in their relationship with you too. And maybe they do, at times, favor your sister. But since you're the one who wrote me, I want to focus on you. Part of living the Christian life is trying to live in harmony with as many people as possible, and that definitely includes your parents.

HONOR YOUR FATHER AND YOUR MOTHER, SO THAT YOU MAY LIVE LONG IN THE LAND THE LORD YOUR GOD IS GIVING YOU.

EXODUS 20:12

One of the most important areas of your Christian growth is to try your best, with God's help, to honor and obey your mom and dad. In only a few short years, you will be out of the house and making most of your decisions on your own. But for now, pull back on the intensity at home and show them honor. This doesn't mean you have to agree with them on everything. It does mean showing them respect and Godly obedience. You don't have to be perfect. But as a growing Christian, you do want to do your best in this particular area. And it's almost a sure thing that less conflict in the house will make everyone happier. So try to honor your parents. If you do, God promises to bring something really good out of it.

A true testimony to a mature spirit is the level of influence one has to keep peace with those around Him.

A STEADY POSITIVE PRESENCE

How can I help my friend keep her faith? Her father has an incurable brain tumor. My friend has always been a strong Christian, but now she's having all kinds of doubts. She's really angry at God, yelling and swearing at Him for ruining her life.

Your friend is experiencing something very normal: Grief. Grief is our response to pain and tragedy. And each person grieves in a different way. When my mom died I wasn't angry at God, but I had an almost overwhelming sense of sadness. Others in my family were angry and, like your friend, took that anger out on God.

Just because your friend is angry at God right now doesn't mean she's going to be angry forever. She doesn't need someone to tell her that her feelings are bad, or that God won't love her if she swears at Him. She's got enough to deal with already without feeling like she's doing something wrong.

Instead, your friend needs to see the love of God through you. Now is the time for you to almost literally be the hands and arms and voice of God. As she deals with the grief of her father's brain tumor, she will need someone like you to just listen to her and be a steady, positive, Christian presence.

It can be very difficult to hear people blame God and shout at Him, but I honestly believe He can take it. Look at Psalm 22, where

David cries out in anguish to God, wondering why God doesn't rescue him from his pain and despair. If God can handle David's anger, He can handle your friend's anger too. I also believe God understands your friend's pain. God knows what it feels like to lose a loved one. Remember, He watched His only Son die on the cross.

So be a living example of God's care and tenderness for your friend. Love her, listen to her, pray for her, and hopefully, she'll find comfort in God's love.

Become the hands, arms, and voice of God.

EVERYTHING WE KNOW ABOUT
GOD'S WORD IS SUMMED UP IN A
SINGLE SENTENCE: LOVE OTHERS
AS YOU LOVE YOURSELF. THAT'S
AN ACT OF TRUE FREEDOM.

GALATIANS 5:14 MSG

I BELIEVE

Can you help me know what to say when someone asks me to prove God is real? I am a Christian, but all I can say is that I believe it with all of my heart.

I don't mean to be blunt, but I don't think you can prove God is real. Some may disagree with me, but God can't be discovered through some formula or by the scientific method. Frankly, the best "evidence" for God's existence is found in something you said in your letter: "I believe it with all of my heart." Your personal experience with God is your "proof" for His existence.

Instead of getting into intellectual arguments with your friends, tell them why you believe and what God is doing in your life. They can argue whether the Lord really made the universe in six days, but they can't argue with your experience.

This doesn't mean Christians should check their brains at the door. Nor does it mean we need to close our mind to the intellectual truths of God's existence. The Bible says we should be able to "correctly explain the word of truth" (2 Timothy 2:15, NLT). And 1 Peter 3:15 says, "Always be prepared to give an answer to everyone who asks you to give the reason for the hope that you have. But do this with gentleness and respect."

So gently and politely encourage your friends to investigate the Christian faith by looking into the life of Jesus. The Bible says Jesus Christ is the "visible image of the invisible God" (Colossians 1:15 NLT). As people learn more about Jesus, they'll gain a better understanding of God's love, creation, and power.

As a young Christian, I began to have doubts about God's existence. For me, a thorough study of the proof of the resurrection helped me to not only believe in my heart about God, but to believe in my head that God created the world and then later entered the world in the person of Jesus Christ. He then died and just three days later rose from the dead. Because of the fact of His life and resurrection, I am forever convinced that there is a God, and that this God not only created the world, but He chose to redeem sinners like you and me so we can spend eternity with Him. Not only do I accept these beliefs intellectually, but I believe them because I have experienced them.

> **I'M A TO Z, THE FIRST AND THE FINAL, BEGINNING AND CONCLUSION.**
>
> **REVELATION 22:13**
> **MSG**

One intimate moment with God eradicates doubts of His existence.

A BATTLE TO WIN

If I'm a Christian, then why do I catch myself doing sinful things, almost on a daily basis? I feel like a total hypocrite, telling others I'm a Christian but then committing sinful acts. How can I change these wrongful ways and totally live for God like I want to?

Actually, you are in very good company. Most Christians I know can identify with you. In fact, the apostle Paul had the same problem you just described. In Romans 7:15-25, Paul described the incredible battle between the spirit and the flesh when he wrote, "I don't understand myself at all, for I really want to do what is right, but I don't do it. Instead, I do the very thing I hate" (v. 15, NLT).

In this section, which I suggest you read, Paul is very honest about the power of sin in his own life. At the end of his thoughts he simply asks, "Oh, what a miserable person I am! Who will free me from this life that is dominated by sin?" His answer is your answer. "Thank God! The answer is in Jesus Christ our Lord" (v. 25, NLT). Paul acknowledges the battle he is in, and he recognizes that Jesus has paid the price for the very sin he fights against.

Here's a story that pretty much sums up our battle against sin. A man went to his pastor with a recurring dream. He said, "Almost every night I have the same dream, a white cat and a black cat are always fighting." The pastor asked, "Which one usually wins?" The man replied, "Whichever cat I feed the most." If we feed the spirit more, we will live by the spirit. If we feed the flesh, the spirit loses.

Go back and read the quotes from Paul that are printed in this answer, and make a commitment to choose to daily thank God for His presence in your life. Then do everything you can to live by the spirit.

Practically speaking, when you're overwhelmed by your feelings of hypocrisy, I suggest you talk to your youth pastor or an accountability partner. An accountability partner is someone you can confide in, and someone you can be honest with about your struggles and your sin. Just being involved in an accountability relationship can help you stay on the right path. An accountability partner can also show you God's grace and forgiveness as you share your life with him or her.

> **ALL WHO ARE LED BY THE SPIRIT OF GOD ARE SONS OF GOD.**
>
> **ROMANS 8:14 AMP**

I appreciate your desire to want to live totally for God. A willingness to repent and sorrow over your sinfulness will definitely help you live out that desire. And God's grace and forgiveness will help you understand you are still loved even when you make mistakes.

Spirit-led choices produce a Spirit-led life.

A NEW OUTLOOK

Do I have to isolate myself from the world because I'm a guy who has impure thoughts about my female friends? I want these thoughts to stop because I hate thinking about my friends this way. I feel like I'm just getting farther away from Jesus. What should I do?

No, you don't have to isolate yourself from the world. But I do believe we can isolate our impure thoughts so they won't control us. A scripture that has helped me is 1 Corinthians 6:18-20: "Flee from sexual immorality. All other sins a man commits are outside his body, but he who sins sexually sins against his own body. Do you not know that your body is a temple of the Holy Spirit, who is in you, whom you have received from God? You are not your own; you were bought at a price. Therefore honor God with your body."

I call this radical respect—not just for yourself, but for the girls you're thinking about. When I'm tempted to allow my thought life to get out of hand, I remember that the person I'm thinking about is a child of God.

Some people who struggle with impure thoughts have not done enough to keep sexually explicit material out of their brains and eyes. It's the old "garbage in/garbage out" principle. If you put impure images and thoughts into your life, then impure images and thoughts will come out. This means not listening to or viewing sexually explicit material via the Internet, movies, TV, CDs, or print media. You still have to live in the world with all its temptations, but you can isolate your mind, body, and spirit from as much impurity as possible, mainly by focusing on things that are good and pure. (See Philippians 4:8.)

I also recommend a book called *Every Young Man's Battle: Strategies for Victory in the Real World of Sexual Temptation* by Stephen Arterburn and Fred Stoeker (Waterbrook). It's full of good, practical advice.

The Bible brings transformation—and your old thoughts go out the window.

DO NOT CONFORM ANY LONGER TO THE PATTERN OF THIS WORLD, BUT BE TRANSFORMED BY THE RENEWING OF YOUR MIND. THEN YOU WILL BE ABLE TO TEST AND APPROVE WHAT GOD'S WILL IS—HIS GOOD, PLEASING AND PERFECT WILL.

ROMANS 12:2

A MORE POSITIVE YOU

Can you help me stop hating myself and wishing I had never been born? I love Jesus very much, but I hate myself. I'm 6-foot-1 and weigh 128 lbs. And I think I'm fat and ugly. I'm told all the time that I'm gorgeous and underweight. I want to believe that, but I don't. My parents are always threatening to take me to the doctor if I lose more weight. I'm scared and don't want to go, but I need help.

I'm worried about you. Even though I've never seen you, I'm guessing that your friends and family are right. Medical charts say a healthy weight for a teen girl your height is anywhere from 144 to 189 pounds. Since you are significantly below the bottom end of that range, a physician would definitely consider you underweight. I'm with your parents on this one; I would certainly take you to a doctor very soon.

I know many people who love Jesus and hate themselves. Some of those people have what we call an eating disorder. One out of five women will at one time in their lives struggle with an eating disorder, usually one of the following:

• Anorexia nervosa literally means "loss of appetite because of nerves." It's an eating disorder associated with a distorted body image. Inadequate calorie intake results in severe weight loss. Some symptoms include refusal to eat or eating in only small amounts, excessive exercise, and an intense fear of becoming obese that doesn't diminish as weight loss progresses.

• Bulimia is an illness characterized by uncontrolled episodes of overeating, usually followed by self-induced vomiting or other purging. Some symptoms include frequent weight fluctuation and throat, esophagus, stomach, or colon problems.

• Compulsive Eating Disorder is characterized by stress eating to satisfy emotional rather than physical hunger. This condition results in overeating and weight gain. Some symptoms include alternating between compulsive overeating and chronic dieting, binging without purging, and feeling out of control with food.

> **HEAR COUNSEL, RECEIVE INSTRUCTION, AND ACCEPT CORRECTION, THAT YOU MAY BE WISE IN THE TIME TO COME.**
>
> **PROVERBS 19:20 AMP**

• It's also possible you have a medical condition that is causing you to lose weight.

Here's what I'd suggest: Go with your parents on this one. See your family doctor, tell him or her exactly how you feel about yourself, and ask for an assessment. The doctor might refer you to a counselor, or maybe to a nutritionist. The Bible is very clear that where there is no counsel people fall, but in the multitude of counselors there is safety (Proverbs 11:14). If you do have an eating disorder, don't wait to get help. It will only get harder to correct your negative self-image.

Trust those God has put in your life to help you build a more positive you.

COMMON PASSIONS

I'm really friendly, but how can I go deeper with those who don't know Christ? I have a lot of Christian friends, which I think is important. But I also want to tell non-Christians about Jesus. My problem is I don't have many non-Christian friends.

I appreciate your zeal and passion to share your faith. When I first became a Christian and started to witness to non-Christians, someone said I needed to "earn the right to be heard." You build relationships with non-Christians just like you do with Christians. Find common interests and areas of their lives where you can relate to them. I've found I can build friendships with non-Christians around hobbies, sports, and common passions.

As you develop a deeper friendship with them, sharing your faith will become a natural part of your relationship. If non-Christians believe you are befriending them only to share your faith, they will often not be as interested in what you have to offer them. I ask myself, "What is this non-Christian friend's greatest need? Is it a good listener? Is it a study buddy? Is it simply someone to sit with at the lunch table?" Many people are open to spiritual things at their point of need. Find their needs and help meet them.

When you find a person's passion, you've reached the door to their heart.

"BY THIS ALL WILL KNOW THAT YOU ARE MY DISCIPLES, IF YOU HAVE LOVE FOR ONE ANOTHER."

JOHN 13:35 NKJV

KEEPING IT TOGETHER

If Jesus drank wine, then is it okay for Christians to drink alcoholic beverages? I have a friend who thinks it's okay to drink, but not get drunk.

Your friend is right about not getting drunk. The Bible is quite clear: "Do not get drunk on wine, which leads to debauchery. Instead, be filled with the Spirit" (Ephesians 5:18). What Paul says here makes a great deal of common sense. You can't walk and live by the Spirit and be intoxicated at the same time. When people are drunk, they're not in control of their lives. The alcohol is in control.

I come from a family where alcoholism is prevalent. I believe there's a biological disposition toward alcoholism. That means if you have blood relatives who are alcoholics there is a much greater chance you could become one. Your body may handle alcohol in a different manner than someone who doesn't have alcohol in his or her family background. I choose not to drink. My three main reasons are named Christy, Rebecca, and Heidi—my daughters. If they see me drink even one glass of beer, wine, or even champagne at a wedding, they may think, *Dad drinks, so I will too.* Then they may find out the hard way that their bodies crave and react differently to alcohol than some other people's do.

But even if alcoholism hadn't been a problem in my family, I'm concerned about setting a bad example. I'm the leader of a Christian organization that helps teens; what would people think if they saw me with a beer? Even if it were just one beer, it would give the wrong impression to many people. As Christians, we need to think about how our actions will affect people who are watching us. Someone somewhere is always watching.

You didn't say how old you are. If you're younger than twenty-one, the answer is clear: It's against the law for you to drink. Period. And anyone who follows Jesus is certainly called to obey the law. Personally, I think the law to not drink until twenty-one is an important piece of legislation to protect young people from great amounts of harm. Many problems occur in the lives of teenagers and their families because of alcohol. And these problems could negatively affect the rest of their lives.

> **WINE MAKES YOU MEAN, BEER MAKES YOU QUARRELSOME—A STAGGERING DRUNK IS NOT MUCH FUN.**
>
> **PROVERBS 20:1**
> **MSG**

Rhonda was one of the student leaders in my youth group; she drove home drunk from a party. Today she is dead, and so are the children and mom in the van she plowed into late one night. And that's only one example.

Now to answer the other part of your question. You're right. Jesus drank wine—at special events like weddings—but He never got drunk. I don't have a problem if an adult (twenty-one or older) has a glass of wine or a beer. But I do have a problem with drunkenness. I've chosen not to drink, and I'm deeply impressed with so many wonderful teens (and parents) who are courageously making a decision not to drink.

Your reputation is like a math equation—it equals exactly what you add to it or take from it.

INDIVIDUAL STYLE

At school, I'm considered a Goth because of how I dress. People judge me by my looks and don't believe I'm a Christian. Do you have any advice on how I can show my faith without giving up how I dress?

Whether or not it's your intention, your choice to dress like a Goth will, unfortunately, stereotype you. By choosing to dress in a Goth style, you will be judged by many because all they know about Goth is Marilyn Manson, Columbine killers, and other Goths the media has put in front of them. Can you be a Christian and dress like a Goth? I think you can.

But remember these two things: People will judge you because of how you dress. And as a Christian, you'll want to check your motives about your appearance. My suggestion is to focus on your relationship with Jesus and let Him mold you into the person He desires you to be. And be open to the possibility of making slight adjustments to the way you dress.

Some say, "Don't judge a book by its cover," yet so many pick up a book and open it because the outside catches their eye.

DECK YOURSELF WITH MAJESTY AND DIGNITY; CLOTHE YOURSELF WITH GLORY AND SPLENDOR.

JOB 40:10 NRSV

PERSISTENT IN PRAYER

How can I help my friend? Last summer I met a non-Christian girl at camp, and we became close. She came from a broken home and had been involved with Wiccan friends. My youth group and I prayed for her and witnessed to her through our own lives. Finally, she accepted Christ. We all continue to pray for her and encourage her. It appeared she was growing in her faith, but recently things took a turn for the worse when she turned back to Wicca and witch-craft. She's my friend, and I want to help her. But I don't know what to do. Sometimes I feel like praying just isn't enough.

Your friend sounds like a confused and troubled person. Your love and care for her will make a difference. Wicca is a powerful religion and lifestyle, which is very popular with young people. Many people who dabble with the Wiccan religion also dabble with forms of witchcraft. My suggestion is to keep on praying and showing the love of Christ, which drew her to the Lord through your youth group.

The mistake some Christians make is when they see someone like your friend leaving the faith and moving to a religion like Wicca, they either give up or begin to put the person down. Jesus Christ died for your friend and loves her just as much as anyone in your youth group. So keep on praying and loving her.

Two books that might help you better understand your friend—and maybe help you lead her back to Christ—are *Witchcraft: Exploring the World of Wicca* by Craig Hawkins (Baker/Revell), and *Exposing Witchcraft in the Church* by Rick Godwin (Strang Communications). Both are available at ChristianBook.com. At the Web site: www.watchman.org/profile/witchpro.htm, you can also learn some basics

A picture of God's love is a prayer to heaven for the life of a friend.

BE PERSISTENT IN PRAYER, AND KEEP ALERT AS YOU PRAY, GIVING THANKS TO GOD.

COLOSSIANS 4:2 TEV

DON'T MISS THE MOMENTS

Am I overcommitted? Next year is my senior year, and I really want to stretch myself. I will have two classes at the local college, and the rest of my classes are Advanced Placement. I will also be part of a volunteer group, possibly president of the drama club, and am editing our school newspaper. On top of all this, I have a job working thirty-five hours a week. I'm excited about doing all of these things, but I'm also scared. I want to prove that I can succeed because I feel these things will help prepare me to do great things for God. But I'm worried I won't be able to handle all of it.

I'm tired just reading your letter! Every involvement you mentioned is wonderful. I do not question your motives, but I am concerned about your method. I think you are taking on more than you can possibly handle. If you try to accomplish all you want for your senior year, I would be very worried about your burning out.

One of my good friends sent me a note many years ago that simply read, "If the devil can't make you bad, then he will make you busy." Don't get too busy doing good things that you miss the joy of celebrating your senior year. Eugene Peterson wrote an incredible paraphrase of the New Testament called *The Message*. A section of Romans 9 that talks about really good people is paraphrased, "They were so absorbed with their 'God projects' that they didn't notice God right in front of them, like a huge rock in the middle of the road. And so they stumbled into Him and went sprawling." Here were some people who had pure motives but wrong methods. They had chosen to be so busy with the work of God that they didn't have time for God.

YOU WILL SHOW ME THE PATH OF LIFE; IN YOUR PRESENCE IS FULLNESS OF JOY, AT YOUR RIGHT HAND THERE ARE PLEASURES FOREVERMORE.

PSALM 16:11 AMP

It would be better to focus and choose fewer good things than be too over-committed and fatigued during your senior year. Many of us try to live life at about 125 percent, and we leave little or no room for the unexpected interruptions of life. For example, during your senior year you will most likely be searching for the right college. What happens if you have a boyfriend, get asked to be a leader in your church youth group, or something happens with a friend who needs you?

You obviously have what they call a type-A driver attitude. Many of the most successful people in the world are type-A. However, if they don't learn to say no to some very excellent possibilities and build margin into their lives, then they are the perfect candidates for burnout and stress-related diseases. People overcommit because they receive a lot of affirmation for all the activities they do. Or sometimes people get in over their heads with activities because they have a poor self-image or are unconsciously repressing some pain in their life by keeping too busy.

I'm not telling you to eliminate any of the great goals you have for your senior year. I'm simply challenging you to reconsider all that you are doing and ask the question, "Do I have room for margin in my life?" (Margin is the space in our life between our load and our limit.) Here is a wonderful passage by Brother Jeremiah as he reflected on his many years of Christian service that reminds the type-A driver in myself to get my priorities straight.

"If I had my life to live over again, I'd try to make more mistakes next time. I would relax. I would limber up. I would be sillier than I have been this trip. I know of very few things I would take seriously. I would take more trips. I would climb more mountains, swim more rivers, and watch more sunsets. I would do more walking and looking; I would eat more ice cream and fewer beans. I would have more actual troubles and fewer imaginary ones.

"You see, I am one of those people who live prophylactically, sensibly, and sanely, hour after hour, day after day. Oh, I've had my moments, and if I had it to do over again, I'd have more of them. In fact, I'd try to have nothing else. Just moments, one after another, instead of living so many years ahead each day. I have been one of those people who never goes anywhere without a thermometer, a hot water bottle, a gargle, a raincoat, aspirin, and a parachute. If I had it to do over again, I would go places, do things, and travel lighter than I have.

"If I had my life to live over, I would start barefooted earlier in the spring and stay that way later in the fall. I would play more. I would ride on more merry-go-rounds. I'd pick more daisies."

Take a break—a day, an hour, a moment—to do everything fun and nothing that's not!

COURAGE TO SHARE

What should my mother and I do? I'm eighteen, and my parents have a terrible relationship. Their hatred of each other is wearing on me physically and spiritually. My mother is a Christian, and my father is Muslim, so I can't get them to see eye-to-eye on things like forgiveness. He has never physically abused any of us, but he flies into rages where he throws and hits things and screams profanities.

You're in a difficult situation. And you're right; hate, rage, and lack of forgiveness really do take a toll on us physically and spiritually. I urge you and your mom to seek wise counsel from a Christian family counselor in your area.

It seems like you're siding with your mom in these conflicts. While I understand that, I'd try to stay clear of their conflicts—unless you feel your mother is in physical danger.

You both need a support system to help change behavior patterns in the family. You may be able to find the help you need in your church. Your dad might also benefit from the loving, forgiving setting of the Christian church.

Even if your parents won't seek help, I urge you to find someone you can confide in. Find someone who can help you avoid repeating your parents' mistakes, to stop the cycle of dysfunction from passing on to the next generation. And work hard to live a life that honors God.

I know a woman who came from a family much like yours. She was eighteen when she went to a Christian university, where she saw another way to live and decided she wouldn't imitate her parents' behaviors. Today she is happily married to a Christian youth worker, and their kids don't have to cope with all the problems she dealt with as a child. My friend decided to give her life wholeheartedly to God and work hard to overcome her childhood scars. You have the same opportunity. It will take a great deal of effort, but it will be worth it.

Finally, never give up praying for your parents. God is a God of miracles.

Your load becomes lighter when you share it with a friend.

THE SPIRIT OF THE LORD IS UPON ME, BECAUSE HE HATH ANOINTED ME TO PREACH THE GOSPEL TO THE POOR; HE HATH SENT ME TO HEAL THE BROKEN-HEARTED, TO PREACH DELIVERANCE TO THE CAPTIVES, AND RECOVERING OF SIGHT TO THE BLIND, TO SET AT LIBERTY THEM THAT ARE BRUISED, TO PREACH THE ACCEPTABLE YEAR OF THE LORD.

LUKE 4:18-19
KJV

REACHING OUT WITH THE HAND OF LOVE

When I move, is there anything I can do to help my sister? I will be moving to the same city as my sister next fall, and I'm concerned about her relationship with God. She is the only person in my family who isn't a Christian. She is an anthropology major and started attending a church by her college. When the pastor found out what she was majoring in, he denied her membership because "she was not in fellowship with them." Since then, she's stopped going to church and doesn't believe in God.

How sad that your sister did not find a loving pastor and an accepting church. It is very possible to disagree on many aspects of our faith and still have fellowship with someone. When you move near your sister, look for a church that you know will love her as Christ loves His Church. He loves the Church not for what we do but rather for who we are. His love is unconditional. There are no strings attached to His love, and that kind of love will draw your sister toward Christ.

Since she was open enough to search for a church before, even though she has been hurt, with your loving assistance she may be able to look again. As for her study of anthropology, there are hundreds of wonderful Christian anthropologists who could relate to her. Do your homework and find someone in your new area who is a Christian yet as knowledgeable as your sister in her field of study.

Frankly, people usually do not come to Christ only out of an intellectual need; they usually are drawn to Christ because of the love shown them by other believers. Disturb your sister's lack of faith with your love, acceptance, and service to her. Since she stopped going to church and believing in God because a pastor did not accept her at his church, so she can, just as quickly, find a solid faith if and when she connects with a fellowship of believers who love her for who she is.

> [LOVE] BEARS ALL THINGS, BELIEVES ALL THINGS, HOPES ALL THINGS, ENDURES ALL THINGS. LOVE NEVER FAILS.
>
> 1 CORINTHIANS 13:7-8 NKJV

When you move, show your sister love, care, and understanding. Earn the right to share your faith with her by showing her you care. You will also be able to introduce her to people who share her intellectual ability but who also have a strong Christian faith.

Love wins out over all the other competitors in every event.

UNCOVER THE TRUTH

How can I get more interested in reading the Bible? I'm not trying to insult it, but I can't read even one chapter. I enjoy books about God, but the Bible puts me to sleep. I don't want to be this way!

You say the Bible is boring, but you like to read Christian books, some of them based on the Bible. I'd guess your problem with the Bible is more centered on how you've been reading it than on what's actually inside.

There are several ways you can read the Bible:

The Bible is a devotional book. You can read the Bible in bite-sized pieces, maybe with a study guide to illustrate its relevance. Since the Bible isn't just any book—but the Word of God—ask Him to reveal the truth of the devotional to you.

The Bible is the history of God's people. You can read the Bible as a history book, telling of God's great work.

The Bible is topical. What does it say about friendships, the end of the world, sexuality, money, or even how to deal with parents? All those topics and many more are in the Bible.

The Bible is poetry. Some of the scriptures are poems from God's people. It's wonderful to be comforted by the Psalms or given good advice from the book of Proverbs.

The Bible is mystery. Parts of the Bible read like a novel. There are battles, love affairs, victories, defeats. There's joy, heartache, wrath, peace. All this and more.

The Bible reveals God. One way God reveals himself to us is through His Word. Although certain parts of the Bible may be more or less interesting to you, it's still the Book that God gave us to better understand His plan of eternal life.

The Bible is eternal. The prophet Isaiah says, "The grass withers and the flowers fall, but the word of our God stands forever" (Isaiah 40:8).

Another great way to get into God's Word is to get involved in a Bible study with other Christians who are excited about it. That excitement can be contagious. Ask someone at your church to get you plugged in to such a group.

Finally, you might consider another Bible translation. Some of today's Bibles are translated or paraphrased into more contemporary language that's easier to read. We recommend The New Living Translation, The Living Bible, Contemporary English Version, or The Message.

Please give the Bible another try. If you read it with an open heart, I don't think it'll be as boring as you think.

FOR THE WORD OF GOD IS LIVING AND ACTIVE. SHARPER THAN ANY DOUBLE-EDGED SWORD, IT PENETRATES EVEN TO DIVIDING SOUL AND SPIRIT, JOINTS AND MARROW; IT JUDGES THE THOUGHTS AND ATTITUDES OF THE HEART.

HEBREWS 4:12

The Bible is the book from which to get your answers for life.

HIS LOVE IN YOU

Is it justifiable to beat up this bully? I'm eighteen, and a guy on the school bus harasses me. It's rarely physical, but sometimes he pushes my back with his foot. I really want to fight back, but instead, I just tell him to leave me alone. What would God want me to do?

Violence isn't the answer to bullying. Ignore him if you can. He's trying to provoke you, and if you don't pay attention to him, he should eventually quit. I know he's hurting your pride, and you want to fight back. But don't give him that satisfaction. That would be stooping to his level. Just try to ignore him, or at least move to another seat as far from him as possible. That's the simplest way to avoid harassment.

If that doesn't work, talk to the bus driver or to authorities at your school. If they can't or won't do anything, then find another way to get to and from school until this problem goes away.

Meanwhile, try to understand what's causing this guy to be so mean. He must be dealing with a lot of emotional pain. Jesus told His disciples to pray for those who insulted them. I'd do the same with this guy. Ask God to soften his heart.

When you let the light and love of God shine through you, those around you see Him in you.

"LOVE YOUR ENEMIES, BLESS THOSE
WHO CURSE YOU, DO GOOD TO
THOSE WHO HATE YOU, AND PRAY
FOR THOSE WHO SPITEFULLY USE
YOU AND PERSECUTE YOU,
THAT YOU MAY BE SONS OF YOUR
FATHER IN HEAVEN."

MATTHEW 5:44-45 NKJV

INFLUENCES OF THE HEART

I feel so far away from God that I sometimes wonder, Am I still saved? I'm a born-again Christian who comes from a good Christian family. But I've gone downhill. I swear and listen to questionable music. I feel awful because of these sins, but it's hard to live the Christian life. I love God, and I don't understand why I keep doing these things. Please help me.

You said "I love God," and I think you mean it. You told me you are born again, from a Christian home, and you want to grow closer to God—all good signs. But here's a quick test anyway to see if you're a Christian: "If you confess with your mouth, 'Jesus is Lord,' and believe in your heart that God raised him from the dead, you will be saved" (Romans 10:9).

Do you believe in your heart that Jesus is Lord? Do you believe that God raised Him from the dead? Do you believe that you love God? If so, then you're saved. It sounds like your struggle isn't with salvation, but with living the Christian life.

The Bible says, "Come near to God and he will come near to you" (James 4:8). If you find ways to draw near to God, He promises He'll come close to you. He'll help you change your lifestyle—including your swearing and choice of music. You don't need someone to preach at you. You need someone to encourage you to draw closer to God and hold you accountable. Read your Bible regularly, listen to God-honoring music, and hang around people who don't swear. Then you'll be able to make some radical lifestyle changes.

I know a teenage girl who was pretty much in the same place as you. She actually moved from one social group to another because she wanted a better peer influence in her life. She also told one of the women working in her youth group that she wanted to be held accountable for developing a stronger relationship with God. They met together for a whole school year in a discipleship relationship. A year later that girl was one of the strongest Christians I knew for her age. I hope you choose the way of discipline and commitment. You won't regret it.

> "A GOOD MAN OUT OF THE GOOD TREASURE OF HIS HEART BRINGS FORTH GOOD; AND AN EVIL MAN OUT OF THE EVIL TREASURE OF HIS HEART BRINGS FORTH EVIL. FOR OUT OF THE ABUNDANCE OF THE HEART HIS MOUTH SPEAKS."
>
> LUKE 6:45 NKJV

The positive or negative experiences you have influence your heart. Choose to build a storehouse in your heart of God's rich goodness in everything you do.

LIVING TRUTH

How can I get my friend to stop using drugs? I've been friends with this guy for about eight months, and even though we don't have much in common, we get along well. But he's on drugs. What should I do?

Your friend needs help. A drug addict must get off the drugs, or his or her life will just get worse. People often take drugs to deaden pain. If your friend is stressed about school or is having family problems, drugs ease his pain, but only temporarily. If anything, drugs can make it worse.

Drug users often forget how to cope with stress. They often move rapidly from the experimental stage to complete dependency. Drugs are scary and dangerous. At first, they may make you feel good. But when their use leads to addiction, the addict must get help to avoid lifelong problems. Your friend is fortunate to have someone like you who cares so much about him.

Confront your friend. Find a place where he can turn for help in kicking his habit. Find former drug addicts who are now clean; they could have a powerful impact on your friend. Pray for him; God can help make him whole again. Ask your youth pastor or pastor for help and suggestions. Your friend is in much more trouble than he may think if he doesn't do something about his drug problem.

Living your life in truth compels others to discover
the freedom they can have in Christ.

A TRUTHFUL WITNESS SAVES LIVES.

PROVERBS 14:25 NLT

PUTTING THE PAST BEHIND YOU

I still have the urge to talk about my past with close friends. Does that mean I haven't forgiven my dad? When I was younger, I was abused by him. He no longer lives with me, so I try to reach out to him through writing letters, but I still feel angry and confused.

It's normal to still feel anger and confusion toward your dad. It's also healthy to feel comfortable enough to talk with your friends about your painful childhood experiences. It sounds like you have come a very long way in being able to deal with your past abuse. All abuse is traumatic, but when your own father is the perpetrator it's even worse. And it can leave very deep emotional scars. You can heal from your wounds, but it might take a lot of work and a long time.

Here are four things to think about:

1. It is not your fault. It's the fault of your abuser. He needs help.

2. Do not suffer in silence. Seek the help you need for healing. Talk to a pastor and/or a professional counselor. Call a hotline like 1-800-NEW-LIFE or 1-800-383-HOPE.

3. You are not alone. There are other teens who have gone through similar experiences. Many of them have sought and found the help they need to live a dynamic life.

4. God cares. Even though at times it may seem like God didn't care about your abuse or that He turned His back, I believe He weeps when His children have been hurt physically and emotionally from an abusive relationship.

Many people don't get to the stage in their healing where they are willing to forgive their abuser. Some learn to forgive but choose not to have a relationship with the abuser. It's just too painful. Yet, some abused people not only forgive their abuser but go on to have a healthy relationship with him or her.

However, keep in mind that this is very unusual. Healing and forgiveness will take a great deal of time. I would strongly urge you to seek continued Christian counseling. Anyone who has been abused needs counsel to stay on the right course of the healing process.

> **"IF YOU FORGIVE SOMEONE'S SINS, THEY'RE GONE FOR GOOD. IF YOU DON'T FORGIVE SINS, WHAT ARE YOU GOING TO DO WITH THEM?"**
>
> **JOHN 20:23 MSG**

Forgiveness can shut the door to the past and pain while opening the door to hope, healing, and a new start.

THE GREATEST FRIEND OF ALL

Every time I quit doing drugs and drinking alcohol, I lose my friends. Because they won't accept me, I eventually go back to that lifestyle. I don't want to give in to this temptation, but it's so hard not to. Do you have any advice?

Yes. Permanently change your friends. If these so-called friends won't accept your desire to be clean and sober, then they're not really friends. The Bible says, "Do not be misled: 'Bad company corrupts good character'" (1 Corinthians 15:33). In fact, I'd call those kinds of people enemies rather than friends.

It's a simple fact that we all become like the people we hang around with. There's both negative and positive peer pressure. Choose your friends wisely and choose friends who will lift you up instead of bringing you down. The Bible talks about a "friend who sticks closer than a brother" (Proverbs 18:24). Search for that kind of a positive influence, and make sure you are searching in the right places—like a Christian club at school or a youth group at church.

I have a college-age friend who was really struggling with drugs and alcohol. He kept trying to quit but kept going back to it. When I asked him what he did for fun, he said he still went to parties with the same friends but tried not to drink or do drugs. I told him if he ever wanted to totally quit, he'd need to leave the party scene and change his friends.

I invited him to the college-age group at our church. At first he turned me down, but after numerous failed attempts at trying to stay away from drugs and partying, he decided to come. He told me recently that he has new friends and is drug- and alcohol-free. You may need to do the same thing.

Also, please don't underestimate the power of addiction. You can change friends and still be under the powerful spell of addiction. If you truly can't quit, seek help right away to get past this addiction. Go to www.christianharbor.com for some suggestions on battling addictions.

When you feel tempted, choose the right side. Christ is in you—ready and able to help you stand strong.

NO TEST OR TEMPTATION THAT COMES YOUR WAY IS BEYOND THE COURSE OF WHAT OTHERS HAVE HAD TO FACE. ALL YOU NEED TO REMEMBER IS THAT GOD WILL NEVER LET YOU DOWN; HE'LL NEVER LET YOU BE PUSHED PAST YOUR LIMIT; HE'LL ALWAYS BE THERE TO HELP YOU COME THROUGH IT.

1 CORINTHIANS 10:13 MSG

LISTEN UP

If I don't know what God wants me to do, how can I follow Him faithfully? I'm confused and unhappy with my life right now. I know God has a plan for everyone, but I don't know what that means for me.

You are not alone. Many Christians struggle with trying to figure out God's will. However, the Bible is quite clear that we can learn much of His will from His Word. The Bible can show you the type of person you should marry. It will teach you about money, relationships, parents, friendships, and the list could go on and on. I would suggest you saturate yourself in the Word. Start reading the Bible and attending Bible studies to find out how to faithfully follow God.

Wise Christian friends can also help you learn what God wants you to do and who He wants you to be. Hang out with people who will challenge you to walk with God. That's how I learn the most, through those friends who help me stay close to God.

Jesus said in the Sermon on the Mount, "Seek first his kingdom and his righteousness, and all these things will be given to you as well" (Matthew 6:33). I think if you seek Him with all of your heart, a lot of your confusion and unhappiness will go away. God doesn't always take away all our pain or confusion, but He does promise to walk with us throughout our lives.

His Words in the Bible, prayer, and praise will speak to your heart, and as you listen, He directs you toward His purposed plan for your life.

**SHOW ME YOUR WAYS, O LORD,
TEACH ME YOUR PATHS.**

PSALM 25:4

ABUNDANT LIFE

Why am I so fascinated with death? For as long as I can remember I've been interested in death. I love to go to cemeteries, and I also love finding out how people died. I love hearing tragic stories and imagining myself dying of a terminal illness. But these thoughts and feelings also make me really sad.

Since this interest in death has been with you for a very long time, I would suggest you talk with a qualified Christian counselor, someone who holds a biblical view of death and the afterlife that secular counselors might not share. Although you didn't mention it in your letter, I am guessing that you had an experience with someone close to you dying or even a trauma that might have caused your fixation on death. It's not necessarily bad to think about death. But since you're obsessed with it, I encourage you to get the perspective of a counselor.

If for any reason your thoughts about death have turned to suicide, then please seek help right away. Call 911 or 1-800-SUICIDE. Your call will help you find help in your area.

Remember that Jesus Christ himself had power over death. Because of His resurrection, He can give us the hope of an eternal home with God in Heaven.

Jesus' very purpose for coming to earth was to give you a full life—and He expects you to fulfill all the days of your life.

THE THIEF COMES ONLY TO STEAL
AND KILL AND DESTROY;
I HAVE COME THAT THEY MAY HAVE
LIFE, AND HAVE IT TO THE FULL.

JOHN 10:10

GOD'S PERSPECTIVE

How do I handle this situation? Teens in my youth group have started calling me "gay" because of the way I talk. I've never had anyone say that before. I feel embarrassed, humiliated, and betrayed by my brothers and sisters in Christ.

I am so very sorry about how terrible and mean these Christians are being to you. You described so clearly how anyone would feel from being treated the way these teens are treating you.

First, acknowledge that your feelings of embarrassment, humiliation, and even betrayal are normal feelings for this situation.

Second, immediately seek help and advice from one of the youth workers you trust and respect.

Third, please do not believe them or doubt your God-given sexuality. I have met people who struggled with homosexuality because they were teased as teenagers. Today they are very unhappy and lack a God-honoring life. If you find the students' teasing has caused you to question your sexuality, please speak with a trusted youth leader or another adult.

Fourth, just because some very misguided Christians in your youth group tease you, do not leave your faith in God. Pray that God would help you find true Christian friends who will support you and lift you up.

God created you to be all He desires you to be. Focus on how He sees you. After all, He made you and loves you.

Keep God's perspective of you before you. You are created in His image—the very apple of His eye.

FOR THUS SAYS THE LORD OF HOSTS: "HE SENT ME AFTER GLORY, TO THE NATIONS WHICH PLUNDER YOU; FOR HE WHO TOUCHES YOU TOUCHES THE APPLE OF HIS EYE."

ZECHARIAH 2:8 NKJV

AN ETERNAL PERSPECTIVE

Why would God let bad stuff happen to us if He loves us so much? A good friend of mine died a few months ago. I've been really depressed and still have a broken heart.

Your letter brought back the hurt of when my best friend died. It's still painful, and I simply don't have an easy answer for you. Here's how I've been coping with it.

Life is a gift. You and I had absolutely no input on when or if we'd be born. And we also don't know when we'll die. God gives us the gift of life, and in His plan, everyone dies. Focusing on what I like to call the "eternal perspective" helps me a great deal.

If your friend was a Christian, you can take comfort in knowing he or she has been transitioned from this life on earth to his or her eternal home with God. Here's what the Bible says about Heaven: "He will wipe every tear from their eyes. There will be no more death or mourning or crying or pain, for the old order of things has passed away" (Revelation 21:4). As much as you want your friend here on earth, you can still find comfort and hope because you know your friend is in a better place.

If your friend wasn't a Christian, you unfortunately won't find much comfort in that eternal perspective. Frankly, it's harder to deal with the death of non-Christian friends because we can't say they've "gone to a better place." But one positive thing can result from the death of a non-Christian friend: It can encourage us to be more determined to share our faith with non-believers, so we can know that they also will have eternal life with God.

Regardless of whether your friend was a Christian or not, you'll want to talk with your youth worker or pastor about your question. Please know it's okay to share your pain, doubts, questions, and even anger with God. You also used the words "really depressed" to describe your feelings. If you're still feeling that way now, you should see a professional counselor.

Finally, you didn't mention whether you're feeling suicidal, but if you are, I urge you not to take your own life. Seek help immediately. Tell someone right away. Suicide replaces a temporary problem with a permanent tragedy. Hold on. If you don't have anyone to talk to, call 911 and explain your situation. Or call 1-800-383-HOPE, 1-800-NEW-LIFE, or 1-800-SUICIDE.

> **YOU DID IT: YOU CHANGED WILD LAMENT INTO WHIRLING DANCE; YOU RIPPED OFF MY BLACK MOURNING BAND AND DECKED ME WITH WILDFLOWERS.**
>
> **PSALM 30:11 MSG**

Before my friend Rob died, I got on my knees and begged God to heal him. For a few months I even thought he would recover, but then he died. I had prayed and even tried to get God to see things my way. But He reminded me, "You will have to trust Me on this. However, through your pain, please don't ever forget what I've promised through Scripture: 'I will never leave you nor forsake you' (Hebrews 13:5 NKJV). I have never said I would keep you or your loved ones free from pain and even death. However, I did promise that I would walk with you through your difficult circumstances."

Turn the volume of God up in your life, and you'll start to notice small joys again.

TRASHING THE TEMPLE

I know that I am underage, but what does God say about smoking? I've been around some Christian adults who smoke.

The Bible doesn't mention smoking. But it does say your body is the "temple of God" (1 Corinthians 6:19). We want to be careful with what we put into our bodies—whether it is nicotine, alcohol, or drugs. I don't know anyone who thinks it's smart to smoke.

I don't question the salvation of those Christian adults you know who smoke, but I do question their decision to keep smoking. They are addicted to a drug called nicotine. It is a difficult drug to get off. The addiction is strong and intense. Most if not all of those people you know who smoke would probably tell you they have tried to quit at some point in their lives. They probably also wish they weren't smokers.

Besides the addiction issue, here are a couple of other concerns for me. Right on the cigarette packages we are reminded that smoking is harmful to our health. Cigarette smoking causes lung cancer, greater heart attack risks, and a bunch of other deadly health problems.

Not only that, but nicotine can lead to addictions with other health risks. According to a former White House drug expert, teenagers who smoke are twice as likely to use alcohol, ten times as likely to use marijuana, and fourteen times as likely to use cocaine and heroin than nonsmokers. In fact, researcher Dr. John Q. Baucom found that 81 percent of teenagers addicted to nicotine will try marijuana. Of young adults who do not smoke, only 21 percent will ever even experiment once with marijuana. For this reason alone, I vote for not smoking.

All evidence tells us that smoking is harmful in so many ways. True, the Bible doesn't say, "Thou shalt not smoke," but it doesn't need to. There are areas where God gives us guidelines and trusts us to decide for ourselves what is best for us. We know we're not supposed to harm our bodies because they are not our own. And we understand plenty about the harmful effects of smoking. Those two facts help us make the decision not to smoke.

And remember: Smoking, drinking, and drugs aren't the only ways to harm our bodies. Habits like overeating or chronic dieting, failing to exercise, and frequently eating unhealthy foods can also damage our bodies.

> I APPEAL TO YOU THEREFORE, BROTHERS AND SISTERS, BY THE MERCIES OF GOD, TO PRESENT YOUR BODIES AS A LIVING SACRIFICE, HOLY AND ACCEPTABLE TO GOD, WHICH IS YOUR SPIRITUAL WORSHIP.
>
> ROMANS 12:1 NRSV

Don't trash the temple, but keep your body presentable before God.

THE POWER OF BEING

Is there anything I can do besides pray? My boyfriend found out his dad's cancer is getting worse. Neither he nor anyone in his family is a Christian, and he has lost hope that anything good will happen again. I try to be there for him, but I feel so helpless.

The answer is in the power of being there. Sometimes there are absolutely no words that can make a difference, but your very presence will often bring the strength needed to get through the day.

I know a man whose wife was dying of cancer. She lay in the hospital almost comatose. Many people from their church came by to offer a prayer, a scripture, and a word of hope. These were very sincere people, but my friend told me, "I appreciated their words of advice, yet most often I could hardly wait for them to leave. However, there was one man who came often. He would show up after working hard all day as a carpenter. His wife had died the previous year. This quiet man would simply come and sit next to me and put his rough hands in mine. Sometimes we would talk, and sometimes we would be silent together." My friend then looked up at me and said, "I never wanted him to leave."

It may not be your words that will make much of a difference, but your presence will say a great deal about your love and the love of God. Now there are times when someone, like your boyfriend, has lost hope and needs to be reassured of God's eternal love. If you read a special verse in the Bible or bring some inspirational words to the family, you may be able to be the person to bring hope back into their lives.

Keep praying for this family and making your presence known. They will definitely appreciate it. I love this challenge from the apostle John at the end of his life. He said, "Dear children, let us not love with words or tongue but with actions and in truth" (1 John 3:18). I think he is reminding us that our actions will speak louder than our words.

> **YOU HAVE BEEN A SHELTER FOR ME, A STRONG TOWER FROM THE ENEMY.**
>
> **PSALM 61:3 NKJV**

Your presence can bring strength to those you love during the hardest times in life.

FAKING IT

How do I tell my friends they're not acting like real Christians without preaching to them? Three of my friends at school claim to be Christians but don't act like it. I don't think they really understand what it means to be a Christian.

You probably aren't the only one who has this problem. All Christians have friends who could be described like your friends. I like the advice that Saint Francis of Assisi used over one hundred years ago when he said, "preach the gospel and, if necessary, use words."

You can sure offer them your advice and confrontation, and in a gentle way you probably should. But your positive Christian lifestyle will do more to bring them to a deeper level of commitment to God than preaching at them.

Imagine for a moment a pyramid. At the bottom or base of the pyramid is what is called the "come and see" level of commitment to God. These are people who may come to church to check out the youth group but do not have a faith of their own.

The next level of commitment is a "casual believer." This may be the level of commitment of your friends. Yes, they are Christians, but they do not take their faith very seriously. Some people call them "nominal" believers. They are Christians, but their actions sometimes don't show it.

The next level of commitment is the "disciple." The disciple has a more mature faith. That is probably where you fit in. There are many fewer disciples than nominal believers and there are fewer nominal believers than come-and-see level people.

Your job is to help your nominal believing friends move up the pyramid to a more committed discipleship life. I think this change happens as they get more involved with Bible study, personal devotions, serving others, sharing their faith, and being in an accountability growth relationship with other disciples.

I would have great patience if I were you, but slowly encourage these friends to get more involved. God is very patient with us, and we must be with our friends. Pray for your friends, and I think you will find opportunity to help them move up the pyramid of commitment.

LIVE A LIFE FILLED WITH LOVE FOR OTHERS, FOLLOWING THE EXAMPLE OF CHRIST, WHO LOVED YOU AND GAVE HIMSELF AS A SACRIFICE TO TAKE AWAY YOUR SINS. AND GOD WAS PLEASED, BECAUSE THAT SACRIFICE WAS LIKE SWEET PERFUME TO HIM.

EPHESIANS 5:2 NLT

Many times your own example is the picture those around you need in order to become more committed.

GOD IS YOUR HELP

What should I do? My parents' marriage hasn't been going well for a while. And now my mom has been talking online with a male friend she met a long time ago. When I approached her about it, she told me everything was innocent and I was crazy to think otherwise. But later I found some evidence that proves it isn't innocent, and I don't know what to do.

You are in a very difficult situation. Some people would simply ignore the possible signs, and others would confront their parent with the information. Both ways of dealing with the problem are complicated and can be messy for your relationship.

Let me first say that you do not have to feel like you are the ultimate savior of your parents' marriage. It's not your fault they are having problems, and it's not your responsibility to make all their problems go away.

Now having said that, after rereading your letter I would imagine you would do what I would probably do, and that is lovingly confront your mother about the new evidence. It is her responsibility to react to what you offer.

She may do it with wisdom and maturity, and she may not. Your job, if this is the direction you choose to go, is to put the information in front of her and reassure her of your love. Let her know that she can go to your pastor or a counselor for help.

Far too many people your age put themselves in the middle of what feels like a game of Ping-Pong, being bounced back and forth with the parents' problems. During this time, be loving and understanding but true to your convictions. You may need an older, wiser person to come alongside you for help, advice, and support. You may want to look to one of your youth workers as a source of strength. They will never take the place of your parents, but they may give you some God-honoring counsel that at this point you aren't getting from your parents.

> **TRUST IN THE LORD WITH ALL YOUR HEART AND LEAN NOT ON YOUR OWN UNDERSTANDING; IN ALL YOUR WAYS ACKNOWLEDGE HIM, AND HE WILL MAKE YOUR PATHS STRAIGHT.**
>
> **PROVERBS 3:5-6**

In the times we don't understand the why, we can always go to the Who—God is our help.

GOD WHISPERS

How can I feel closer to God? Lately my personal relationship with Christ has deteriorated, almost to the point of nonexistence. I've tried praying, but it hasn't been working. I'm lost and have no idea how to become closer to Him again.

I wish I had an easy answer or a specific formula for you to follow that would help you find your path back to God. There are no easy solutions. However, there is a wonderful scripture that I hope you will see as a great promise: "Come near to God and he will come near to you" (James 4:8). The beauty of God is that His ways are not always our ways. Some people come back to Him through prayer, others by being involved in serving through a mission project. I know a person who went camping out in the beauty of God's creation and while sitting at a lake in the mountains felt God's presence in the trees and water. He made his peace with Christ that day sitting by the lake.

A student named Cara wrote me a while ago about the same problem you are having. She then told me it wasn't until she became involved in a small group at her church where she started hanging out with strong and authentic Christians that her faith became real to her. I don't know what you need, but the scripture is so true that as we draw toward God, He will draw toward us. In the Old Testament there is another promise that can spur us on: "You will seek me and find me when you seek me with all your heart" (Jeremiah 29:13). God's presence and His power are offered to us as we focus our lives in His direction.

Again I don't know your specific situation, but when I was in college I was in a similar situation as you. I wanted to be closer to God, and I felt far away. One verse in the book of John turned me in the right direction. "Whoever has my commands and obeys them, he is the one who loves me. He who loves me will be loved by my Father, and I too will love him and show myself to him" (John 14:21). Here's the principle I learned from those words of Jesus. No matter what I feel about God, my job is to obey Him. When I obey and follow Him, it shows Him that I love Him. In return, as I obey, He promises to reveal himself to me.

THE SOUND OF THE WINGS OF THE CHERUBIM WAS HEARD AS FAR AS THE OUTER COURT, LIKE THE VOICE OF GOD ALMIGHTY WHEN HE SPEAKS.

EZEKIEL 10:5 NRSV

Soon after learning that verse I broke up a negative friendship and went on a mission trip to Mexico. Both acts of obedience helped me get back on the right path and sense God's presence in my life. When you are quiet before God, when you look deep into your soul, what is it that you believe God is whispering to you? Obey His whisper and come back to Him. He will do the rest.

He is always speaking, but you hear Him only if you're listening.

HEART CONNECTIONS

Do you have any advice for me? I have moved around a lot because of my parents' jobs, so I'm not in a youth group anymore. Right now it seems I have no one to lean on. I sometimes attend church but don't have a true church home. I don't understand why God is letting this happen to me.

It is very important that you find "community." Community is a sense of belonging. We all need it. Very few people can thrive in their faith without community. Even though you move frequently, you can still try to find a close group of Christian friends.

Throughout Scripture, God tells His people to share fellowship with other believers. In the Old Testament the theme is often about being "connected" to a group of believers. The New Testament says we should not "give up meeting together, as some are in the habit of doing, but let us encourage one another—and all the more as you see the Day approaching" (Hebrews 10:25). The word picture from the mouth of Paul is that we are all important parts of the body of Christ who need each other very much. (See 1 Corinthians 12.)

Let me challenge you to find a youth group and church that fits you. No group will be perfect, and it will take time to feel connected. In order to speed up the process—join a small group, attend a retreat, or spend one-on-one time with a student leader or youth worker in your church.

When I was a youth pastor, Kristi, a girl in my group, had a similar problem because her parents moved often. The first day I met her she put out her hand, greeted me, and said, "I've just moved to this area. I've been checking out youth groups and want to commit to this one. I will probably move in the next couple of years so I want to get involved right away."

I was impressed with her attitude. Kristi jumped right in, and after a few months she really was a major part of our group. I'm sure our youth group wasn't exactly like her last one, but she put it behind her and got involved. I suggest you follow Kristi's example and find a sense of belonging with Christians in your area.

> **JUST AS LOTIONS AND FRAGRANCE GIVE SENSUAL DELIGHT, A SWEET FRIEND- SHIP REFRESHES THE SOUL.**
>
> **PROVERBS 27:9 MSG**

Make a point to include others in your group, and you'll find your group will grow.

HOPE RESTORED

Surely God knows how much hurt you've been through, so why would He send you to hell if you commit suicide? I heard that even if you're a Christian and commit suicide, you go to hell.

Whenever a church or youth group has a Bible study or discussion on the subject of suicide, the first question seems to be about hell. At one time a major Christian denomination taught that if a person committed suicide, they would be sent straight to hell. This denomination has since backed off from that thinking, but the idea is still on the minds of many.

The Bible is very specific on several important subjects. Where it is specific we are called simply to believe. It is specific and clear, for instance, on heaven and hell—not how they relate to suicide but rather to our relationship with Jesus Christ. Romans 10:9-10 says, "If you confess with your mouth, 'Jesus is Lord,' and believe in your heart that God raised him from the dead, you will be saved. For it is with your heart that you believe and are justified, and it is with your mouth that you confess and are saved." It is clear that our salvation depends on our relationship with God, not on a specific action.

Again, and as mentioned above, the Bible is not clear on the subject of suicide. Nevertheless, I strongly believe it is never God's will for someone to commit suicide. For a person contemplating suicide, the issue is not hell, but finding the hope to get past their pain and live the abundant life Christ offers. God doesn't promise a life free of pain, but He does offer to never leave us nor forsake us (Deuteronomy 31:8). When a person attempts suicide he or she has basically lost all hope. But Christ is a restorer of hope.

You didn't say whether you were considering suicide yourself, but if you are, I strongly urge you to choose life instead. Tell a trusted adult—a parent, a teacher, a pastor—right away what you're going through, and they'll point you to the help you need. Or call one of the following numbers: 911, 1-800-SUICIDE, 1-800-NEW-LIFE, or 1-800-383-HOPE.

> O PRISONERS WHO HAVE THE HOPE; THIS VERY DAY I AM DECLARING THAT I WILL RESTORE DOUBLE TO YOU.
>
> ZECHARIAH 9:12
> NASB

Jesus Christ is the restorer of your hope.

MAJOR DIFFERENCES

What is a cult? I belong to the Church of Jesus Christ of Latter Day Saints (Mormon Church). In a past issue you said that Mormonism is a cult. When I looked up cult in the dictionary it says that a cult is a group that follows a leader. Catholics follow the pope, Lutherans follow Martin Luther, and Mormons follow the teachings of Christ from the Bible and the Book of Mormon. Doesn't this make everyone part of a cult then?

If you're looking at the Webster's dictionary definition of "cult," you are absolutely right. A cult in its simplest meaning is a system of religious worship. But to Christians, a cult is a religious group with beliefs outside the mainstream teaching of the Christian faith. I have very good friends who are Mormons. We have a wonderful common bond in similar family values and other issues surrounding our lives. However, we must agree that the Mormon Church and mainstream Christianity are quite different on a few key points.

Here are two points to ponder:

1. Joseph Smith: Was he a prophet or not? Did God send the angel Moroni to deliver the Book of Mormon to Joseph Smith, as Mormons claim? Obviously, Mormons believe that Joseph Smith was a prophet and that the Book of Mormon is a holy book. Christians

do not believe Smith was a prophet or that the Book of Mormon is holy. Christians believe the Bible—and nothing else—is the only true Word of God. Mormons believe they have a "new scripture," sort of a nineteenth-century addition to the Bible. That's a major difference in our faith and practices.

2. One of the other major differences is salvation. Mormons believe salvation (going to Heaven) comes through good works and that all people will spend eternity on some level of a multi-storied heaven. The level will be determined by the scope of each person's good works. The Christian view is radically different. We believe that salvation is a free gift of God's grace for all who believe and accept Jesus Christ into their lives (Ephesians 2:8-9; John 14:1-6).

> **JESUS TOLD HIM, "I AM THE WAY, THE TRUTH, AND THE LIFE. NO ONE CAN COME TO THE FATHER EXCEPT THROUGH ME."**
>
> **JOHN 14:6 NLT**

There are several other major differences between Mormonism and Christianity such as our view of God, the Bible, and sin. So it is very safe to say the teaching of the Christian faith and Mormonism are different at some of our core beliefs.

When disagreements arise, it is better to focus on saving the friendship rather than determining who is right or wrong.

IT'S NOT YOUR DECISION

What can I do besides pray for my dad? I was using my dad's computer and looked at his Internet history files and found porn sites. I think this is disgusting. It's actually not the first time I've seen this type of stuff on his computer. I thought it had stopped, but I was wrong.

It's frightening just how many men are jumping into the scary pit of Internet pornography. Your dad needs help, and most likely, if confronted, he will experience incredible shame. Experts tell us that the power of pornography to rule our minds is as intense as a drug or alcohol addiction.

The Bible is clear when it comes to immorality. "It is God's will that you should be sanctified: that you should avoid sexual immorality" (1 Thessalonians 4:3). The word "sanctified" literally means "to be set apart" or holy. We are challenged to be different from the world.

It's important to point out that the New Testament Greek word "pornia" is translated as "immorality." This is the same root we find in the word "pornography." The Bible is clear: We must avoid any type of sexual immorality including the use of Internet pornography. Another Scripture tells us to "flee from sexual immorality" (1 Corinthians 6:18).

Your dad is probably hurting as he mixes the temptation of his sin with the desire to avoid pornography. So what should you do? I don't believe it's your role to help your dad work through his problem with porn. But since you've found the evidence, you should confront him—in love, not in anger—with what you've found. I'd suggest saying something like this, "Dad, I found more history of porn sites on your computer. I'm sure you don't want to keep going in that direction. Here are a couple of organizations who might be able to help." Suggest Pure Intimacy (www.pureintimacy.org), Sexaholics Anonymous (www.sa.org, 1-800-339-0222), or Sex Addicts Anonymous (www.sexaa.org). You might also encourage him to talk to a pastor or Christian counselor.

I think you also must express your love and pray for him. If you continue to see evidence that he's still involved with pornography, talk with a counselor or pastor who could help you deal with the issue. In these kinds of situations, we can and must reach out to our loved ones, but they are the ones who must ultimately make the decision to change.

> **SO LET'S AGREE TO USE ALL OUR ENERGY IN GETTING ALONG WITH EACH OTHER. HELP OTHERS WITH ENCOURAGING WORDS.**
>
> **ROMANS 14:19 MSG**

Love, encouragement, and forgiveness work together to turn the lives of many toward God's best.

THE WOMAN QUESTION

What does the Bible say about women in ministry? I am a girl, and my relationship with God is very good. Next year I am going to college, and I feel God leading me into some sort of youth ministry. I have told this to a few of my male friends, and they told me their opinions. They said they believe women shouldn't go into ministry because it is a man's job. I don't know what to do.

You asked a very controversial question. The church has been divided on this issue for centuries and especially since the middle part of the twentieth century. Most Christians, because of the world-wide Catholic Church, Orthodox Church, and conservative evangelical church, still have a practice of not "ordaining" women as pastors. What we call mainline protestant churches, many Pentecostal churches, and progressive evangelical churches are more apt to ordain women.

All churches would agree that women do most of the work in the church. Typically women are the ones who care for the poor and visit the sick and pray for those in need. More women run the nurseries, teach Sunday school, and organize church events. Whether or not a church allows a woman to be ordained as a pastor, few people would disagree with me that women are key leaders in the church. In previous generations and even during the time the Bible was written, many people thought women were inferior to men. Fortunately, that was not the opinion of Jesus. Jesus brought what was a very radical thought in His day, that male and female were all one in Christ. Some of the Rabbis looked at women in the days of Jesus as no better than dogs. But that was not Jesus' view.

Back to your question. Christians have basically two opinions on this issue. The first opinion agrees with some of your friends that women should not go into the ministry. The most often quoted section of scripture for that view is found in 1 Timothy 2:9-15. One of the verses reads, "I do not permit a woman to teach or to have authority over a man; she must be silent" (1 Timothy 2:12).

A few verses earlier in 1 Timothy 2:9 Paul writes, "I also want women to dress modestly, with decency and propriety, not with braided hair or gold or pearls or expensive clothes . . ." There are many Biblical references which apply specifically to the context of the day. This first opinion tends to say that women should not be pastors or elders but views the scripture about braided hair and clothes in the historical context of the day.

Personally, I have a great deal of respect for people who hold this view if they have the Biblical integrity to also hold as literal all the other historical views. There are churches that are thriving and love the Lord who hold this view.

Others, including myself, believe that God uses both women and men to do the work of the Lord. In my personal experience, some of the finest ministry people I know are women. Their love and passion for God and willingness to be used by Him are a real inspiration to me. But again you asked the right question, "What does the Bible say?" I believe that the New Testament released women to do any job in the church a man can do.

Obviously, on the mission field women have been leading churches for years. I believe that in God's eyes "there is neither male nor female" when it comes to being used by Him to minister. I'm so glad that Godly women and men are influencing my three teenage daughters in their youth groups.

On a personal note, I have been deeply moved by the wonderful preaching of Anne Graham Lotz. Her father is one of my heroes, Dr. Billy Graham. He has often been quoted as saying, "Ann is the finest preacher in the Graham family."

> **THERE IS NEITHER JEW NOR GREEK, THERE IS NEITHER SLAVE NOR FREE, THERE IS NEITHER MALE NOR FEMALE, FOR YOU ARE ALL ONE IN CHRIST JESUS.**
>
> **GALATIANS 3:28 NKJV**

The debates will continue on women in ministry for centuries. Both sides quote scripture, and both sides want to follow God's direction. This is where you will want to seek the wisdom of wise counselors and definitely seek God's direction and will for your life. Pray the prayer of James, when he says, "If any of you lacks wisdom, then ask God, who gives generously to all" (James 1:5).

A simple willingness to follow the leading of the Lord has opened doors and made dreams a reality in the lives of many women.

A FATHER WHO LOVES YOU

I hate my dad. What can I do about it? About three months ago my dad and I got into a big argument. He said some mean things, and I was really hurt. My parents are divorced, and I've always had a lot of hatred toward him. He treats me like I'm a mistake. In fact he tells me I am. When I confronted him about it, he made me feel terrible.

No father should ever tell any child he or she is a mistake. If your dad said that, I think you should write him a letter and tell him how much he hurt you. Even if he doesn't respond in the way you would hope, at least he knows how you feel. Don't use the letter to "rip on Dad." Just let him know how much pain his words caused. I hope your dad will see the light and apologize.

I want to make sure you know how your Heavenly Father feels about you: "A father to the fatherless, a defender of widows, is God in his holy dwelling. God sets the lonely in families, he leads forth the prisoners with singing; but the rebellious live in a sun-scorched land" (Psalm 68:5-6).

Your heavenly Father loves you. He is proud of you, and He wants the best for you. When you know you have a loving Heavenly Father, it's a bit easier to lower your expectations for a less than perfect dad. Here's my advice on how to handle your earthly father.

Walk in his shoes. What was his family life like when he was growing up? What are his pressures and problems? Is there anything that you have done or said to contribute to the break in the relationship?

I know a woman who was physically and emotionally abused as a child by her mother. When she learned how depressed her mother was, it didn't take all her pain away, but it did help her understand why she had a poor relationship with her mom.

> **SO BE MERCIFUL (SYMPATHETIC, TENDER, RESPONSIVE, AND COMPASSIONATE) EVEN AS YOUR FATHER IS [ALL THESE].**
>
> **LUKE 6:36 AMP**

Seek counsel and support. When you don't have a lot of support at home, it is even more important to be active in your church youth group. There, you can hopefully find a sanctuary of love and support. No one can ever replace a parent, but your "extended" family can meet some of your needs for positive relationships. Ask your youth leader or pastor for some suggestions on how to deal with your dad.

Work on your relationship with your dad. Your dad will always be your dad. You may still need to forgive him for his divorce and his poor relationship with you before your situation can improve. As you grow and mature, you may end up taking steps toward reconciliation with him.

Stay close to your Heavenly Father. God can and will help fill the void in your life. Jesus told the disciples to pray to "Abba," the Hebrew word for "Daddy." God wants us to approach Him in the way a child would run to greet his father. Go to your Heavenly Father often and ask Him to be intimately involved in your life.

You always have a Father you can turn to in God.

BUILDING A POSITIVE DIFFERENCE

How do I get rid of this excess baggage and start to live my life and enjoy it? I've been rejected a lot in the past and the mocking has left scars. Because of these scars, I now have this huge social problem. I can't get words out to talk to people. I've been reading my Bible and praying a lot, but it just seems to be getting worse.

I believe you are starting in the right direction with prayer and Bible reading. Both talking with God and reading His Word will give you the guidance and healing you will need from the spiritual perspective.

Let me first tell you what not to do from the mocking and scars. Don't do what a young teenage girl from Michigan did just a few weeks ago. She was a "Gothic" who read books on witchcraft. She was often teased and mocked by her peers. Even some Christians who should have known better taunted her. One day in one of her low moments she killed herself. Obviously she was a troubled person. Somehow she chose a very permanent solution to a temporary problem.

When people have scars from rejection they can either turn it around for good or they can act out their pain with destructive behavior. Suicide is only one of the many negative destructive behaviors. Other types of destructive behaviors include drugs, sexual promiscuity, violence, withdrawal, eating disorders, cutting, and on and on. Negative destructive behaviors never make the pain permanently go away. They just suppress it for a while and usually cause even more pain and often more rejection.

YOU WILL KEEP IN PERFECT PEACE ALL WHO TRUST IN YOU, WHOSE THOUGHTS ARE FIXED ON YOU!

ISAIAH 26:3 NLT

You are doing it right. You are taking your pain and trying to make a positive difference in your life. Keep on reading your Bible and praying. As you grow closer to God you will experience more and more of His presence and peace in your life. Also find friends and adults who will lift you up and not mock you. Although a church youth group is far from perfect, there are people who are like yourself in those groups who want to overcome their problems and have a sincere desire to grow closer to God. Finally, don't forget to seek out wise counsel from someone who could help you with your past. The biblical principle is clear, "Where there is no counsel, the people fall; but in the multitude of counselors there is safety" (Proverbs 11:14 NKJV).

Keep on building that safety net around your life and watch the growth take place.

THANKFUL HEARTS

How do I act like a good Christian without judging others or putting myself above everyone else? Lately I've realized that I religiously judge people too harshly. I try not to, but it's really hard.

Just this morning I read a verse that I actually wrote down in my journal. It sure challenged me, and perhaps it's for you also. "Before his downfall a man's heart is proud, but humility comes before honor" (Proverbs 18:12).

When I humble myself before God and confess my sins, it is extremely difficult to judge anyone else. For me, as the years have gone by I've become humbled by my own sinfulness and failures, and I've found it easier to be patient with others.

Here are some strong words from the mouth of Jesus. "Do not judge, or you too will be judged" (Matthew 7:1). I find that when my judgment mode kicks in it is often because of envy or jealousy or my own insecurities.

Every day when I pray I spend time praising God and exalting Him to His proper place in my life, thanking Him for all He has done for me, and frankly confessing sins. The daily confession of sins has a way of humbling us and keeping us from judging. Praising and thanking Him also reminds us that it's about Him and not about us.

When we put God in His proper place in our lives there isn't much room for judgment.

After all, without the sacrifice of Christ we are all sinners and fall very short of the glory of God. You may have a friend or family member who has a really gross sin in his or her life, but compared to the perfection of our Savior, you and I aren't one ounce more righteous than that person.

HE LEADS THE HUMBLE IN WHAT IS RIGHT, AND THE HUMBLE HE TEACHES HIS WAY.

PSALM 25:9 AMP

I have a friend who told me he used to be a very judgmental person. Actually, he was quite a bit better off than some of the members of his family whom he often judged. One day he decided that it was God's job to judge and not his. As an act of the will, he gave his judgmental feelings about his family members over to God.

Two things happened almost immediately. First, he felt released to love and accept his family, which brought him a sense of peace. Second, his relationship with his family improved greatly because somehow they sensed he wasn't being as judgmental of them anymore. Some of his family members actually became Christians after they felt less judged.

Work on relinquishing your judgmental attitude to God, and you will no doubt be a more content person, not to mention the powerful impact you might have on those you were judging.

A heart full of humility has no room for judgment.

THE GIFT OF CHOICE

Why does God let things like murder happen? I'm strong in my faith, and I trust God. But I want to know why bad things happen to good people. I know everything happens for a reason, but why this?

God chose to not make us puppets. He gave us a will to decide life on our own. He never promised to take away bad things in our lives; He promised to stay with us through the hard times. God chose to have us live in a fallen world where there is murder and injustice. And He uses people like you and me to help make it a better world.

You have asked a question that is often on the mind of many of us. In fact there was a best-selling book a few years ago titled *When Bad Things Happen to Good People*. There is a shooting on a school campus, and people want to know why. The holocaust takes place during World War II, and we want answers to this absolute tragedy. A wonderful young man or woman is disabled for life because of a freak accident, and we all look to God for insight, if not to blame Him.

You asked a very important question, yet I cannot find a satisfactory enough answer for you. I want to tell you that there is a simple verse in the Bible that will take all the bad things and make them good. I can't find a simple answer in the Scripture. Romans 8:28 says, "We know that in all things God works for the good of those who love him, who have been called according to his purpose." I believe that scripture to be truth, yet it is still difficult to answer the question why.

The ultimate answer is that we are not God and no one really knows why bad things happen to good people. All I can say is that in times of major tragedy I honestly believe our God deeply cares for our pain. He wept at the death of a friend (John 11:35), and He weeps with us in our pain and tragedy. For some reason He chose to give us not only a will of our own but also a world that is involved in a spiritual battle between good and evil.

From reading the Scripture, we know that God will ultimately triumph in the end. But for now evil reigns alongside good in this fallen world. Part of developing a mature faith in Christ is being able to live with the tension of some of the uncertainties in life while maintaining the certainty that God knows what He is doing even when we don't have easy answers to important issues like your question. Do all you can to fight for justice and leave the rest up to God.

> **"TODAY I HAVE GIVEN YOU THE CHOICE BETWEEN LIFE AND DEATH, BETWEEN BLESSINGS AND CURSES. I CALL ON HEAVEN AND EARTH TO WITNESS THE CHOICE YOU MAKE. OH, THAT YOU WOULD CHOOSE LIFE!"**
>
> **DEUTERONOMY 30:19 NLT**

Trust God to do what is right and just from the eternal perspective.

THE BEST IS YET TO COME

What do I do? I thought my life was supposed to get better since I accepted Christ into my life. It seems to have gotten worse. Recently I went to a Christian camp. They told me that if I handed my life to Christ I would notice great results because I let God into my life. So I did what they told me. I stopped drinking and tried to devote myself to God. But ever since my friends noticed that I don't drink, they've stopped hanging out with me. They never answer my calls and never invite me places. I haven't heard from them in weeks. Please help me.

Your life did get better from an eternal perspective. As you allow Christ to control your life you will notice a difference. This is the way I figure it. Do you want the Savior of the world leading your life or you? I don't know about you, but I would rather have God's presence in my life than try to do it all on my own.

However, if your friends at camp told you giving your life to Christ would make everything better, they accidentally misled you. The change in your relationship with God is immediate from a spiritual perspective, and that is most important. But sometimes other parts of our lives do get more complicated.

When I became a Christian at age sixteen, I actually ended up changing my group of friends because of their somewhat negative influence on my life. If your drinking friends have quit calling, that may end up being a good thing even if it is painful at the moment.

WHATEVER IS BORN OF GOD OVERCOMES THE WORLD; AND THIS IS THE VICTORY THAT HAS OVERCOME THE WORLD—OUR FAITH.

1 JOHN 5:4 NASB

For your eternal relationship with God you made the right decision, but He never promises that our lives on earth will be easy. Two promises in the scriptures come to mind. God said, "I will never leave you nor forsake you" (Joshua 1:5). No matter what happens God promises to be there for you. Even if right now your friends are not calling, God has promised to ALWAYS be present in your life.

Another wonderful promise of God is found in Psalm 37:4 NLT, "Take delight in the Lord and he will give you your heart's desires." Your job is to delight in God, and His job is to keep His promise of bringing to you your heart's true desire. When it comes to your future marriage partner, vocation, friendships, and lifestyle, you will want to make sure that you give those areas of your life over to God, because He has promised to give you the guidance you need to live a life with Him. Remember, He never promised to take away all hardships or problems. But He did say He would be there with you to help fight your battles of life.

Our job is to be faithful to God. His job is to show us a new and greater way of living our lives on earth.

YOUR OWN STYLE

My friends, whom I love very much, have a habit of making comments about my clothes. I'm careful to wear modest clothing, and nothing I wear is unusual. It really hurts, though, because when I buy something I like to be sure that I'll wear it several times. But I find myself being greatly affected by my friends' opinions when I pick out what I want to wear in the morning.

My mom says they're just jealous or looking for ways to boss me around because I have more clothes than they do. But I get really embarrassed when they say anything in public. How can I handle this criticism while still being able to enjoy my own taste and style? I'm frustrated that it's having such an impact on me.

Your friends are wrong to tease you about your clothes. I don't know if they are jealous or if they have just gotten into a habit of making fun because they see that it bothers you. I'm impressed that you are willing to not go with the crowd and you dress the way you feel most comfortable and with modesty. You are to be commended, not ridiculed.

Here's what I would do. I would take each friend aside and tell him or her one-on-one how uncomfortable you feel when others tease you about your clothes. I wouldn't do it in anger, but rather casually and sincerely. No one likes to be teased about clothes, and no one who dresses with modesty and class deserves to be teased.

In today's generation, you should be praised. If your friends continue to tease you, or if it becomes malicious, then it may be time to find new friends.

When you stand up for God, He stands up with you!

BE STRONG AND COURAGEOUS. DO
NOT BE AFRAID OR TERRIFIED
BECAUSE OF THEM, FOR THE LORD
YOUR GOD GOES WITH YOU; HE
WILL NEVER LEAVE YOU NOR
FORSAKE YOU.

DEUTERONOMY 31:6

FEAR NOT

How can I support my mom? My father left our family when I was young, and my mom remarried. I really liked my stepfather, and I was crushed when he died recently. My mom has started dating, and she hopes to get married again one day. I want to support her, but I'm scared that she will either meet someone who will neglect me like my real dad did or die before I can get to know him better.

For all you've been through, your feelings are certainly very normal. I encourage you to find support as you're going through this difficult time. Talk with an adult you trust and share your feelings and fears. You need someone who can help you get through this time of terrible loss.

As difficult as it is to lose another dad, please know that your heavenly Father will always be close to you. In fact, your heavenly Father says to you through His Word: "I will never leave you nor forsake you" (Joshua 1:5). Read this verse often. Let it become God's personal message of comfort to you.

As for the possibility of your mother remarrying, you need to let her know what you're feeling right now. Obviously, the decision to

> **YOU WILL KNOW THAT I AM THE LORD; THOSE WHO WAIT FOR ME SHALL NOT BE PUT TO SHAME.**
>
> **ISAIAH 49:23 NRSV**

remarry is totally up to her. Even so, she deserves to know how you feel. So try to be honest and open with her.

If your mom does remarry, your "new dad" will most likely be quite different from the one you just lost. But you should be encouraged. She apparently did an excellent job choosing your stepfather, so hopefully she will do the same if she meets someone again.

One final thought. Try not to think about all the "what if" questions. Don't spend time worrying about what may happen if your mom remarries. Hand your fears over to the God who promises to take care of you (Matthew 6:25-33).

In the face of hope—an earnest expectation of God's very best—fear runs and hides.

PRACTICE AND PERSEVERE

How can I put God first and live for Him more than I live for myself? Sometimes when I'm praying or reading the Bible, I start thinking about other things I'd rather do, and I know that's not good.

We all have those times of being unfocused. I have two words for you: practice and persevere. Practice the presence of God. That means practice staying focused on God. If you are praying, and you last two minutes, good for you—next time go for three.

Have you ever practiced a sport or a musical instrument, or rehearsed for a school play? When you begin practicing, it's difficult to imagine that you'll ever achieve your goal. But through practice you end up achieving it. So start with a simple goal and build on it.

Now practice isn't always easy, is it? That's where perseverance comes in. It's the ability to stick with your practice even when all you want to do is give up. So why persevere? Because God promises that good will come out of it.

Personally, I do better when I make a daily appointment to talk with God and read Scripture. I'd encourage you to make your own regular "appointment with God." Write down a specific time to meet with God, the amount of time you'd like to spend with Him, and some specific things to do during your time with God (such as prayer, a devotion, or reading Scripture).

> **For this very reason, make every effort to add to your faith goodness; and to goodness, knowledge; and to knowledge, self-control; and to self-control, perseverance; and to perseverance, godliness.**
>
> **2 Peter 1:5-6**

Other helpful ideas:

1. Find a quiet place that allows you to avoid distractions. Get away from the TV and loud music. If it helps, and the weather's right, go outside. Sometimes nature is a great place to feel God's closeness. Or maybe you like praying in a comfortable chair in the house. Just find a place that helps you concentrate and keep focused.

2. Find a time that's right for you. I can't do my devotions or pray late at night. I've been known to fall asleep in the middle of my own prayers!

3. Be creative. Some people focus better by writing out their prayers. Or you could sing or listen to worship songs. As for reading Scripture, try digging deeper into a passage's meaning by reading it in three or four different versions. You'll find different versions online at biblegateway.com.

God never divides or subtracts from your life, but only adds and multiplies.

PROFANITY IN CLASS

Some of my teachers cuss in front of me and it really bothers me. One teacher even uses phrases like, "Oh my God" in class. Should I tell them how uncomfortable their language makes me feel?

If it continues to bother you, and you feel compelled to talk with your teachers, then in the most non-preachy and nonjudgmental attitude possible, have a talk with them. Some people in your situation would just let it go or check it off as part of living in a fallen world.

However, the truly courageous thing to do is very politely tell them that it bothers you. I might say something like this: "Mr. Jones, I am really learning a lot in this class. Thanks for all your hard work. I do have one request, and I am not being judgmental; but is there any way you could cut down on your use of profanity in this class?" Keep it short and simple.

By the way, you have the Bible on your side. The Scripture is quite clear when it says, "You shall not take the name of the LORD your God in vain" (Exodus 20:7 NKJV).

God is honored when you are valiant for the truth.

LET THE HEAVENS BE GLAD, AND LET THE EARTH REJOICE: AND LET MEN SAY AMONG THE NATIONS, THE LORD REIGNETH.

1 CHRONICLES 16:31 KJV

GOD APPROVED YOU

How can I get my dad to love me? Most of the time, I'm a happy seventeen-year-old girl who's living with a passion for God. But there are times when my dad says harsh things to me, and I get so upset that I hurt myself physically—scratches and bruises. My dad is very uninvolved in my life, and he makes me feel like I will never be good enough for him. I haven't been able to figure out what will make him proud of me.

I want to deal with two issues from your note to me. First, I am very concerned about the way you are handling the pain and problems in your life. When people physically scratch, bruise, cut, bite, or harm their bodies, they are reacting to the problems in their lives in an unhealthy way.

You do have reason to be very frustrated with the problems with your dad, but hurting your body is only going to make things worse. This week, make an appointment with a counselor at church or school and tell him or her you want to learn how to deal with your problems more effectively. Tell the counselor you have been hurting yourself and that you don't want to react to your hurt this way anymore. If you are like most people who cut themselves or hurt their bodies in other ways, they truly want to stop but sometimes simply can't help themselves. Get help now before it progresses.

Now let's talk about your dad. It sounds like he has some problems himself. The best thing you can do is tell him exactly how you feel. Tell him what kind of relationship you dream about having with him. Explain how you feel when he is so harsh. Let him know that you want him to be proud of you and that you sometimes wonder if he really loves you.

Bringing these problems out in the open is a mature way to deal with them. You'll want to time this conversation well, so that your father won't feel as threatened. For example, don't tell him these things in the heat of a battle. Wait for a tender moment or save up some of your money and take him to one of his favorite places to eat.

If you feel too uncomfortable talking directly to him right away, write him a note and then talk. Keep from focusing on how bad he is doing and focus on the kind of relationship you wish you had.

You can't fix your dad. He needs to face his problems and seek help, and he may simply not be willing right now. Don't let that keep you from taking positive action, though. Talk to him, and then do whatever you can to help yourself. He may or may not change. But with God's help, and with the help of a counselor, you can discover love and self-acceptance.

> **YOU ARE A CHOSEN PEOPLE, A ROYAL PRIEST-HOOD, A HOLY NATION, A PEOPLE BELONGING TO GOD, THAT YOU MAY DECLARE THE PRAISES OF HIM WHO CALLED YOU OUT OF DARK-NESS INTO HIS WONDERFUL LIGHT.**
>
> **1 PETER 2:9**

God loves and accepts you for who you are—if He can, you can, too.

RESPONSIBLE DECISION-MAKING

What should I do now? My best friend recently told me he is gay. He said he wasn't "out" yet, though I kind of knew even before he told me. We are both Christians, and I had wanted us to remain best friends.

When he suddenly stopped going to church and youth group activities, I got really concerned. So I told our youth leader about his secret, thinking she could help me convince him to come back to church. I told my best friend that I'd shared this information with our youth leader, and now he's mad and won't talk to me. Did I do the right thing?

Your friend isn't talking to you because he feels deeply betrayed. It's safe to assume he's terribly embarrassed at having his secret shared. If I were you, I would apologize to him for talking to your youth pastor without first telling him you were going to do it. Hopefully, your apology will help restore your friendship.

After apologizing, explain to your friend that you were concerned when he stopped going to church. Try to find out why he pulled away from the church, and listen carefully to the reasons he gives you. Finally, encourage him to come back to church.

Please don't give up on your friend. You can disagree with a person's lifestyle and still show care and concern for the person. And just because someone tells you they are a certain way doesn't mean they aren't open to change.

Here are some points to guide you as you try to help your friend through this difficult time:

- Do what you can to help in light of God's Word and God's love.
- Be caring and loving no matter what he says to you.
- Introduce your friend to positive role models.
- Find a way to address possible abuse. Many people who struggle with sexual identity have been sexually or physically abused.
- Discuss the biblical teaching on healthy sexuality.
- Encourage openness.
- Confront carefully.
- Check out www.exodus.to for more information and support.

> **DON'T LOSE YOUR GRIP ON LOVE AND LOYALTY. TIE THEM AROUND YOUR NECK; CARVE THEIR INITIALS ON YOUR HEART.**
>
> **PROVERBS 3:3**
> **MSG**

The challenge in making decisions is accepting responsibility for them.

THE RIGHT CROWD

What can I say or do to become one of the popular kids? I'm new to my school, and I want to become popular. I think I can be: I have a good sense of humor, and I always make people laugh.

And I know of another new girl who is not even pretty, and she is going out with the cutest guy in school. So I figure I could become popular too. I go to a Christian school, and while nobody is ever left out, there is definitely a "popular" group.

I think your words capture the feelings of many high school students. While you say nobody gets left out at your school, I sense that you still feel left out. After all, you are sure you're not part of the popular crowd. For whatever reason, you simply don't feel like you're part of this popular group—and you long to be.

But think about this: If you do become part of that crowd, there are many others who won't be there, right? They would feel left out just like you do now. When people are striving to be included in a popular group, someone always ends up being excluded.

Instead of trying to edge your way into some exclusive group, seek to be inclusive. Just try to be friends with as many people as possible. Avoid labeling others as "popular" or "unpopular."

If you try to simply be a good friend to anyone who comes your way, you'll soon be able to enjoy friendships with a number of people—and not just the exclusive few.

One who shows himself friendly to everyone gains many friends.

NO ONE HAS SEEN GOD AT ANY TIME; IF WE LOVE ONE ANOTHER, GOD ABIDES IN US, AND HIS LOVE IS PERFECTED IN US.

1 JOHN 4:12 NASB

A FAITHFUL FRIEND

What should I do? My best friend isn't a Christian. I know you're supposed to have Christian friends, but I can't stop being friends with her. We do things together, and we always have fun. But when I try to talk to her about God, she says she's just not ready to commit to Him. I take her to church every Sunday. She says she has fun, but I just want to make sure she becomes a Christian.

Being a Christian doesn't mean you have to give up all your non-Christian friends. Non-Christians are not terrible people. On the contrary, some of the most generous and loving people I know are not Christians. I learn from them, enjoy their company, and am challenged by their questions. I encourage you to keep relationships with non-Christians because through your loving example, they may come to know Jesus.

But to be a growing believer, you also need friends who will challenge you spiritually. Make sure you're developing strong relationships with believers who can build you up in your faith. I must also caution you to be aware of your relationships with non-Christian friends. Be sure those friendships aren't leading you to do, say, or think things that are contrary to your Christian values.

As for reaching out to your friend, it sounds like you're doing a fine job. You bring her to church, you pray for her, you share your life with her. Sometimes we have to earn the right to be heard before talking with others about Jesus. John the apostle gave some wonderful advice when he said, "Dear children, let us not love with words or tongue but with actions and in truth" (1 John 3:18).

You can also witness to your friend by doing a Bible study together. I suggest going through the gospel of Mark and studying the life and teachings of Jesus. This way she'll gain a better understanding of who Jesus is.

> **"AND I, IF I AM LIFTED UP FROM THE EARTH, WILL DRAW ALL MEN TO MYSELF."**
>
> **JOHN 12:32 NASB**

Never forget that God cares more for your friend's soul than you do. Your job is to be faithful to your friend. God's job is to draw her to himself.

What an awesome thought that He would use you to influence your friend for eternity!

PRAY ANYWAY

When do you stop praying for someone? If I prayed for everyone who asked for prayer, I would have a never-ending list. When can I take them off? I know God knows our wants and needs before we go to Him, but shouldn't I specifically mention people and their situations? Even if people do change, they still need prayer so they won't fall back into their old ways. What do I do?

People handle their prayer life in different ways. I like to keep a journal. I list prayer requests and write down names. From time to time, I go back through the list and pray for people I haven't thought of for a while. Often, going back over the journal will motivate me to pray for them.

A very important part of prayer is two-way communication. In our moments of solitude, we can listen to the whisper of God. Most of the time it comes in the form of an idea or impression through our minds. During times of silence, God will often prompt a name to pray for or a situation to pray about.

I hope you will pray consistently for the people close to you. I became a Christian when I was sixteen, and I prayed for my father to make a commitment to Christ. My prayers for him were passionate and constant throughout the rest of high school and on into college. After several years, however, I prayed for him less and less. I'm not sure if I lost faith or just got lazy. But after many years God has brought me great joy because my dad recently became a Christian.

Don't give up too quickly on your prayers. God hears all of them, but He answers on His timing, not ours. Eventually we do get an answer from Him. In 1 Thessalonians 5:17 KJV, we are commanded to "pray without ceasing." When we pray for others, we're assured that God is watching over those we care about. I can think of no one better to take care of those we love.

THE EYES OF THE LORD ARE UPON THE RIGHTEOUS (THOSE WHO ARE UPRIGHT AND IN RIGHT STANDING WITH GOD), AND HIS EARS ARE ATTENTIVE TO THEIR PRAYER.

1 PETER 3:12 AMP

God listens with an attentive ear when you pray.

GOD'S RICH LIFE

I have accepted Jesus into my heart several times, and each time I did, I really felt like I wanted to change my life. But when I'm outside of church, I don't feel that way anymore. I'm not ready to give up things for Jesus. I don't think I love Him enough to want to change my life. I believe you should live life to the fullest, and Christianity is only concerned about life after death. I find myself wanting to give up on Christianity and just live life the way I want to. Please give me some advice.

I think you might have some mixed-up messages about Christianity. Jesus told His disciples, "I have come that they may have life, and have it to the full" (John 10:10). That doesn't sound to me like the Lord is only interested in life after death.

Christianity is much more than the assurance of eternal life with God after we die. The best possible way to live life to the fullest is to live your life with Jesus as your master. You'll find He's not "the great killjoy." On the contrary, He wants to lead you in a life of fullness and adventure. And He will do that as you seek to obey His will. If you trust that God's plan for you is best, you'll find it's better than anything you could have come up with on your own.

You aren't alone in your struggle to give up the things of this world. The apostle Paul said this about his life: "I have the desire to do what is good, but I cannot carry it out. For what I do is not the good I want to do; no, the evil I do not want to do—this I keep on doing. Now if I do what I do not want to do, it is no longer I who do it, but it is sin living in me that does it. So I find this law at work: When I want to do good, evil is right there with me. . . . What a wretched man I am! Who will rescue me from this body of death? Thanks be to God—through Jesus Christ our Lord" (Romans 7:18-21, 24-25).

Notice that Paul answered his own dilemma when he thanked God for rescuing him and giving him eternal life through Jesus. You can do the same. Don't give up on your faith. Seek out a strong group of Christians to help you enjoy God's best for you each and every day of your life—beginning right now.

GOD IS ABLE TO MAKE ALL GRACE (EVERY FAVOR AND EARTHLY BLESSING) COME TO YOU IN ABUNDANCE, SO THAT YOU MAY ALWAYS AND UNDER ALL CIRCUMSTANCES AND WHATEVER THE NEED BE SELF-SUFFICIENT [POSSESSING ENOUGH TO REQUIRE NO AID OR SUPPORT AND FURNISHED IN ABUNDANCE FOR EVERY GOOD WORK AND CHARITABLE DONATION].

2 CORINTHIANS 9:8 AMP

God wants you to have the very best life!

SMALL STEPS IN THE RIGHT DIRECTION

I know I should be standing up for God and my beliefs at school, but for some reason I always get scared. What can I do to not be so afraid?

Many people feel the same way you do. It's not easy! I encourage you to take "baby steps." As you think about taking your faith to school, start small. Join a campus Bible study so you can meet regularly with Christians. After you take a small step in the right direction, my guess is you'll feel stronger to take a stand for God.

When Dave, a member of my youth group, became a Christian, he was shy about sharing his faith. I encouraged him to meet and pray with one of the students in our youth group a few days a week before class. Out of that time of prayer, they decided to start a Bible study at lunch.

They invited a few of their friends, and it just kept growing. By the time the year ended, sixty students were meeting at lunch for prayer and fellowship. Dave was one of the leaders and was even asked to pray at the school's graduation ceremony.

Dave is a perfect example of a person who was as reluctant as you to bring his faith to school, yet with "baby steps" he was able to become more comfortable with showing his faith on campus.

If you would like more information on claiming your campus for Christ, check out the Web site everyschool.com.

Take your faith to school (and everywhere you go) one step at a time.

GIVING ALL DILIGENCE,
ADD TO YOUR FAITH VIRTUE,
TO VIRTUE KNOWLEDGE,
TO KNOWLEDGE SELF-CONTROL,
TO SELF-CONTROL PERSEVERANCE, TO
PERSEVERANCE GODLINESS,
TO GODLINESS BROTHERLY KINDNESS,
AND TO BROTHERLY KINDNESS LOVE.

2 PETER 1:5-7 NKJV

BUILDING TRUST

I need your help. I like to go out with my friends, but my mom usually won't let me. I'm a good kid. I don't drink, smoke, or have sex. I get so angry at her. I end up sitting home while all my friends are out having fun. Most of my close friends understand, but I'm losing other ones, not to mention pushing away potential boyfriends because she never lets me do anything. What can I do?

Parents are in the "protection business," and I think your job is to earn their trust. As you show yourself trustworthy, they'll most likely begin to trust you more. When you're trying to get along with your parents, remember this:

1. Nobody sent them to parent training school. They are still trying to figure out how to be parents. Remember, they're people, and they make mistakes too.

2. Your parents are running scared. They may never tell you this, but when it comes to raising you, they are a bit frightened. After all, it's pretty easy to blow it as a teenager. They know this because they probably made some mistakes growing up.

3. Parents often express care and concern in overprotective ways. This doesn't mean they are always right, but it probably does mean they really love you.

4. Your parents could be going through their own identity crisis. Just like you, they have their own issues to deal with, and sometimes they take their stress out on the family.

Most criticism has at least a grain of truth in it, so look for ways to listen, hear, and respond humbly to your mom's critique. First of all, you say you don't drink, smoke, or have sex. Do your friends? Is it possible that your mom is concerned because she sees things in your friends that she's afraid will rub off on you?

CHILDREN, OBEY YOUR PARENTS IN ALL THINGS, FOR THIS IS WELL PLEASING TO THE LORD.

COLOSSIANS 3:20

NKJV

If you truly believe your mom is totally unreasonable, I suggest you get a third person to hear both of your concerns. This could be your pastor, youth worker, or even a trained counselor. You just need someone who will offer you and your mom unbiased guidance and advice. Whatever happens, in the midst of the battle, try to cut your mom some slack. She's probably doing the best she can.

A heart of genuine obedience gains a trustworthy reputation.

TURN IT AROUND

I'm really frustrated with all the gossiping I hear at school. I don't want to participate in these conversations, but I don't know if I should speak up. What would you do?

Gossip is like a wildfire. It gets out of control and spreads quickly. The Bible places gossip along the same line as greed, sexual perversion, and even murder (see Romans 1:29). Just like we can murder someone with a gun, we must be careful not to "murder" someone with our tongues. Gossiping is a sign of a low self-image, a really bad habit, or both. The best thing to do is not join in. But, when you're put in a situation where people are gossiping, you do have a few options:

1. Walk Away.

2. Tell your friends that gossiping is wrong and refer to the old adage, "If you can't say something nice, don't say anything at all."

3. Turn the conversation around by either saying something positive or by changing the subject.

Words are very powerful, and our tongues are hypocritical. James 3:9 says, "With the tongue we praise our Lord and Father, and with it we curse men, who have been made in God's likeness." Ephesians 4:29 tells us to say things that are "helpful for building others up according to their needs, that it may benefit those who listen." Your positive example will be the best way to keep your friends from gossiping.

If you have nothing good to say about someone, say nothing at all.

SO SPEAK ENCOURAGING WORDS TO
ONE ANOTHER. BUILD UP HOPE SO
YOU'LL ALL BE TOGETHER IN THIS,
NO ONE LEFT OUT, NO ONE LEFT
BEHIND.

1 THESSALONIANS 5:11 MSG

VS. EVOLUTION

I go to a public school, and in our science classes we learn about the theory of evolution. How do I handle it when my teachers try to tell me I evolved from a gorilla?

I had a similar problem with one of my college classes. I remember the frustrations I had, but going back to study what I believed helped me through it. You, too, have to make a choice on how you're going to handle this situation. You can take science as a home school course, while continuing to take other classes at your public school. Or, you can look for a different teacher in your school who shares your beliefs and ask to be switched to that class.

However, don't consider these options without seriously thinking about staying in the class and studying twice as hard as you need to for the grade. I've seen students who read their text, listen to lectures, and then study books that support a different view. They also spend time talking with pastors about creation.

You can also try to argue with the science teacher, but my experience says that usually doesn't work as well as investing the

> **GOD FORMED MAN OUT OF DIRT FROM THE GROUND AND BLEW INTO HIS NOSTRILS THE BREATH OF LIFE. THE MAN CAME ALIVE—A LIVING SOUL!**
>
> **GENESIS 2:7 MSG**

extra time to study both sides and coming up with a well thought out belief of your own. The important thing in this situation is to explore the theories of evolution and creation for yourself so you may be confident in God and your belief in Him.

God is the maker and creator of all.

HEALTHY INFLUENCES

I wanted to go see a PG-13 movie with some friends, but my parents said no. They said what goes into my mind comes out in my actions. But they watch R-rated movies. If as Christians we're supposed to glorify God, why can they watch R-rated movies, but I can't watch PG-13 movies?

For Christians today, it's not an easy decision when it comes to films and their ratings. I'm sure you would agree that just because a film is rated PG-13, that doesn't mean it's Sunday-school clean.

Should your parents as Christians ever watch an R-rated movie? That decision is between them and God. Sometimes parents can seem hypocritical in their ways, but usually they truly have a justification for the decisions they make. If I were you, in the least judgmental way possible, I would ask them how they make their viewing decisions as adults and as Christians. You may learn something, and in just a few years you will have to make those same decisions on your own.

You are rapidly moving from childhood toward adulthood, and one of the major parts of your mom and dad's job description as parents is to teach you to discern what types of influences are healthy and not healthy for you. Whether we like it or not, parents are in the "protection business." I'm glad your parents care enough to make a decision.

There is room for negotiation with your parents. But I encourage you to practice patience and respect when you do disagree with them. And try to learn something from their decisions. In a few years you'll be deciding what movies you watch—and God should be included in those decisions.

When in doubt—leave it out.

FINALLY, BROTHERS, WHATEVER IS TRUE, WHATEVER IS NOBLE, WHATEVER IS RIGHT, WHATEVER IS PURE, WHATEVER IS LOVELY, WHATEVER IS ADMIRABLE—IF ANYTHING IS EXCELLENT OR PRAISEWORTHY—THINK ABOUT SUCH THINGS.

PHILIPPIANS 4:8

PERMANENT MARKINGS

What does the Bible say about body piercing and tattoos? Would it be wrong to get a tattoo even if it's something as innocent as a ladybug?

You have raised a very controversial topic. The Bible really doesn't speak directly about piercing or tattooing, but both have become very popular today. Many people will choose to pierce and tattoo.

When you are an adult, what you decide is really between you and God. However, my wife and I have chosen not to allow our own teenagers to get anything more than their ears pierced while they live in our home. And they aren't allowed to get a tattoo—even if it is just a ladybug. But we have good reasons behind our rules.

Sometimes teenagers, and adults too for that matter, make decisions they regret. Occasionally, my job as a parent is to delay the decision until adulthood. Recently, my family was looking through my junior high and high school yearbooks. We spent more time laughing at the hairstyles and clothing then anything else in the books. I must admit that what I thought was cool when I was sixteen now looks awful.

We can change our hairstyles and our clothes, but a tattoo is permanent. Today you like ladybugs, but what about ten years from now when ladybugs are out or the tattoo phase of your life is over? The decisions you make today will affect you for the rest of your life.

Before you decide to permanently mark your body with piercings or tattoos, ask yourself the following questions:

1. What statement am I making with this piercing or tattoo?

2. Does it honor God?

3. How might this decision affect me ten years from now? twenty? thirty?

Once you have answered these questions, get the opinion of your parents and pastor. They might not always be right, but it is wise to seek the counsel of others before making a permanent decision.

> **WISDOM WILL COME INTO YOUR HEART, AND KNOWLEDGE WILL BE PLEASANT TO YOUR SOUL.**
>
> **PROVERBS 2:10**
> **NRSV**

When you follow the wisdom of God, you are assured the right choice.

THE ETERNAL GIFT

My best friend claims to be a Christian, but she thinks all she has to do is be a good person to go to Heaven. I don't really know how to talk to her about this subject because she's supposedly already saved. Could you please give me some advice?

Definitely don't put your friend on the defensive. Since she is your best friend you have the opportunity to influence her in positive ways. I would invite her to church often and try to get her involved in a small group. If that doesn't work, ask her to consider doing a one-on-one Bible study with you.

I would suggest you start with the basics—beginning with Ephesians 2:8-9, which says, "It is by grace you have been saved, through faith—and this not from yourselves, it is the gift of God—not by works, so that no one can boast."

Your local Christian bookstore can help you find a workbook to explore the basic truths of faith together. Start with something simple and practical to her life. You may find that she will open up best in a smaller setting than a church service or function. Keep praying for your friend, and remember

> **THE WAGES WHICH SIN PAYS IS DEATH, BUT THE [BOUNTIFUL] FREE GIFT OF GOD IS ETERNAL LIFE THROUGH (IN UNION WITH) JESUS CHRIST OUR LORD.**
>
> **ROMANS 6:23 AMP**

that God cares more about her than you do. Trust Him to work through you. Don't be afraid to share your heart with her.

The gift of salvation cannot be purchased, earned, or bought, but only accepted by faith.

NO STING

I have a problem with death. I know there's a wonderful side to it, but I can't get past the fear I have of someone I love dying. The thought completely overwhelms me. What can I do?

Even as Christians, death can be frightening. No matter how much we know or believe about the subject, it's still unsettling.

You will never get used to the idea of a parent, friend, or loved one dying. It will happen, and it's never easy. When a person who's close to us dies, we experience grief. This is a normal part of living.

My advice is that you familiarize yourself with many of the great Bible passages and promises about death and Heaven. A favorite of mine is Psalm 23:

The LORD is my shepherd, I shall not be in want. He makes me lie down in green pastures, he leads me beside quiet waters, he restores my soul. He guides me in paths of righteousness for his name's sake. Even though I walk through the valley of the shadow of death, I will fear no evil, for you are with me; your rod and your staff, they comfort me. You prepare a table before me in the presence of my enemies. You anoint my head with oil; my cup overflows. Surely goodness and love will follow me all the days of my life, and I will dwell in the house of the LORD forever.

God's promises can keep our minds at peace. One day, we all will experience the pain and grief that accompanies the death of a loved one. Here are a few points to remember about grief:

1. It's normal to grieve. You must grieve before you go on with life. Never be afraid to cry or recognize your hurt. These feelings and emotions are normal.

2. Grief takes time. You will not get over your pain instantly. The ache may be with you for a long time.

3. Talk about it. As we share our sorrows, we at times receive strength and mutual support.

4. Find comfort in the Bible. Read Scriptures about peace, hope, and victory over death. A few suggestions besides Psalm 23 are Psalm 46, John 14, and Romans 8.

> **HOW WE THANK GOD, WHO GIVES US VICTORY OVER SIN AND DEATH THROUGH JESUS CHRIST OUR LORD!**
>
> **1 CORINTHIANS 15:57 NLT**

Right now, you are doing what you need to do by facing your fear of death. Keep on facing your fear. Don't be afraid to talk about it with people you respect. A conversation with a counselor or even your parents is a good place to start.

While it's reasonable to fear the process of dying, we, as Christians, have great hope for what comes next—eternal life in Heaven, no more suffering, no more fears, no more death.

Death is stripped of its power when you accept Jesus.

TIME TO REST

Is working on the Sabbath wrong, even if I attend a church service that day? My job requires me to work on Sundays, but my boss has arranged my hours so I can attend worship.

Today we live under God's grace rather than the Old Testament law (Romans 6:14). Let me explain. In the Old Testament, the law said the Sabbath had to remain holy. In fact, it's one of the Ten Commandments (Exodus 20:8-11) of the Old Testament. An orthodox Jew would not have even thought about working on the Sabbath. But today, we live under the principle of New Testament grace. Even working on Sundays falls under the banner of Christ's grace.

However, if at all possible I vote for taking the day away from work to focus on worship, rest, family, and friends. Our culture has made Sunday a day to cram in more sports, more work, and more shopping. I honestly believe this lifestyle causes us to not slow down enough.

Think of your life as a car with a tank full of gas. By the end of the week, it's out of gas. You need to drop by the gas station for a fill-up. You go, go, go all week long and you, well, run out of gas—and not just physically. You need to slow down and refill your spiritual, emotional, and physical "tank." You need time to rest and exercise. And you need time specifically for God. A restful, worshipful Sunday is a good time for this to happen.

But what about if you have to work on Sundays? Well, I would suggest you find a day or even a night after school where you schedule "Sabbath time." Make sure you plan your weeks with this time always open. Write it into your planner. Get your home-work done in study hall. And then, get busy not being busy. Relax, go for a run, spend time with God, and have fun with your family. Even if it's not on Sunday, you need time to stop for a fill up.

> **IN A CERTAIN PLACE HE HAS SAID THIS ABOUT THE SEVENTH DAY:**
>
> **"AND GOD RESTED ON THE SEVENTH DAY FROM ALL HIS WORKS."**
>
> **HEBREWS 4:4**
> **AMP**

There is a good reason the Bible says that on the seventh day God "rested from all the work of creating that he had done" (Genesis 2:3). He took a day off to replenish himself, setting an example for us as well.

Even God took a day to relax!

THE LITTLE WORD "NO"

What's the line between Christian charity and being taken advantage of? I've been blessed by two high-paying summer jobs and come from a slightly wealthier family than my friend from church. Because of this, he often makes remarks about how "rich" I am. When he goes on mission trips he regularly asks me to sponsor him—and I have a few times for hundreds of dollars.

I do it because I feel I should use my blessings to help others. The problem is that he keeps asking me for donations and doesn't do much for our friendship except when sponsorship time comes. I fear I am being taken advantage of. Is he my friend? How can I respond to him?

You are learning a life-long lesson about relationships, giving to God, and living with pure motives. My advice is to give your tithe and offering to God. (Period!) People who give a part of their income to God tend to live much more faithful lives as followers of Jesus Christ. People who find joy in giving are in fact oftentimes more joy-filled. Try your best to keep your focus on the One you are giving to in the first place.

If your "friend" is using your generosity only as a way to receive monetary assistance, then I doubt if he is much of a friend in the first place. If your "friend" makes inappropriate remarks about the wealth in your family, then I question his sincerity. You will have to be the judge of that issue. Make sure, as in any potential conflict, that you discuss your feelings with this person. Tell him how you feel. If certain comments have hurt you, then tell him in the nicest of ways.

There are many times when God uses friends to support friends on mission experiences. In fact, in the New Testament and even today, entire churches have supported the missionary efforts of people they had relationship with through previous ministry and friendships. This is normal and natural. You will want to learn that your giving is not connected to what you receive back in a friendship.

> **EACH ONE MUST DO JUST AS HE HAS PURPOSED IN HIS HEART, NOT GRUDGINGLY OR UNDER COMPULSION, FOR GOD LOVES A CHEERFUL GIVER.**
>
> **2 CORINTHIANS 9:7 NASB**

Give to God. When you give, ask God to give you pure motives. Pray about all the money you give and who to give it to. If you make more money, then you will be able to give more money. Don't feel obligated to support anyone, but do it with joy and know that because you have more money, there is a good chance that you will get asked more often.

You may have to relearn one of the first words out of your mouth as a child: "No." You could say something like, "I wish I could support every worthy effort that comes my way, but I can't. I will pray for you." I think when you tell your friend your feelings and as you seek God's plan for your giving, your particular question will be answered.

Give to God with pure motives.

FIND HEALING

When I was young I was emotionally and physically abused by my alcoholic mother and her boyfriends. Because of this my dad and his new wife took me in at the age of six. They know there were problems, but I've never told them details. Now, I am experiencing lots of flashbacks of what happened and things I saw around me. What can I do?

Seek the help and advice of a professional counselor. Don't delay. If you don't know who to go to, then ask your pastor, youth pastor, or a school counselor, and they can give you a referral. The Bible is clear, "Where there is no counsel a people fall, but in the multitude of counselors there is safety."

You were a victim of abuse, and there will be times when the trauma will come back into your life full force. Although what happened to you is always close to the surface of your life, now is the time to speak with someone who is a professional in helping you deal with these issues. Don't try to repress them or make them go away. Work through it. Before freedom may come more pain. But for the sake of your emotional, spiritual, relational, and even physical life, do what it takes to find healing.

I know people who have had traumatic experiences like yours and don't do anything about it until they are much older. What they didn't take into consideration was that their abuse would affect their marriage, children, and relationship with God. That's why now is the time to get help.

Your decision to talk with your dad and stepmom might be best made once you have talked to a counselor. However, with this major issue going on in your life, I wouldn't wait too long to share your painful memories and experiences with your family.

> **HE HEALS THE BROKENHEARTED AND BINDS UP THEIR WOUNDS [CURING THEIR PAINS AND THEIR SORROWS].**
>
> **PSALM 147:3 AMP**

One last thing, please know that God cares deeply for you and grieves when you grieve. Keep close to the Lord. Talk with Him. Don't be afraid to approach Him with anything on your mind. My prayer for you is that the nail-scarred, loving hands of Christ will protect you and cover you with His presence and His peace.

When you can finally let go, you can embrace freedom.

SPIRITUAL WORLD

Christians don't believe in magic and are warned of its dangers. But things in the Bible like Moses turning his staff into a snake seem like magic to me. How can I understand this better?

Great question. Actually, I am not an authority in this field, so I would suggest that you talk with your pastor or someone who knows a great deal more than I do. Here is my best shot at your question.

The world you and I live in is more than it appears. The Bible calls it the "flesh and the spirit." I believe there is a spiritual world that we do not see in the flesh. There are times when God uses miracles to present His truth and blessing to the world like in the case of turning Moses' staff into a snake. There are literally hundreds of miracles in the Bible. I believe that God is still actively doing miracles for His glory today. Moses was not performing magic; instead he was experiencing a miracle of God.

There is also an evil spiritual world. The Bible says that Satan is the leader of this world. He is described as deceiving, evil, dark, and in conflict with God's world. Cleverly, Satan uses "miracles and some magic" to confuse humankind.

The Bible talks about a spiritual battle that is constantly taking place between good and evil. That is why I tell everyone not to dabble in the occult, witchcraft, Satan worship, or even Ouija boards. You never want to take the risk of dabbling in something that Satan could use to take you away from God.

As for the issue of magic, some people may disagree with me, but some magic is harmless. I know a wonderful Christ-follower who practices what he calls, "illusions." Some of the kinds of magic you see on TV by famous people are nothing more than entertainment and illusions. Yet, some of those famous people do dabble in very dark practices. You just have to look at the person and the fruit of his or her life.

ABSTAIN FROM ALL APPEARANCE OF EVIL.

1 THESSALONIANS 5:22 KJV

Pray for discernment. Seek the advice of people who can give you more information. Just don't do anything that would compromise your relationship with the living God, who we know the Bible says does win the ultimate spiritual battle in the end.

If it gives you a bad feeling—it probably is bad. Let God's wisdom speak to you—and listen.

CALLING GOD'S NAME

Is saying "Oh my God" a sin? I say that, and I can't kick the habit.

Whenever you're in a crowd, and you hear someone call your name, don't you turn around to see if the person is talking to you? Of course you do. The same goes for God. When people say, "Oh my God," they're calling on the name of their Creator. Let me give you a scenario.

Jim: "Oh my God!"

God: "Yes, Jim."

Jim: "Oops! I didn't actually mean You, God."

God: "You called My name. I thought you wanted to talk with Me."

Jim: "Actually, it was just an expression I used to exclaim surprise. No offense, but I didn't mean to call upon You, God. I just said God like some people would say the word gosh. Uh, maybe I should use a different word than Your name from now on."

God: "Whenever you call My name, I will be listening."

The Bible clearly tells us not to take the name of God in vain. The Ten Commandments say, "You shall not misuse the name of the LORD your God" (Exodus 20:7).

Do you mean to abuse the name of God when you use that popular phrase? Probably not. But whenever we say the name of God, we are calling upon Him to listen to us and respond to our prayer.

When we say "Oh my God" as an expression of surprise, we've cheapened the name of our Creator. Using His name in a casual manner trivializes our relationship with God. In the Old Testament, one of the names for God is Yahweh. This name was so special to the Hebrew people that they would only whisper it. The Jews felt God's name was so holy they wouldn't even personalize it.

Christians have a personal relationship with God only because of our relationship with Jesus. But we are still called to respect the name of God and hold it in reverence. Far too many people say "Oh my God." Do everything you can to kick the habit.

> "TEACHER, WHICH IS THE MOST IMPORTANT COMMANDMENT IN THE LAW OF MOSES?" JESUS REPLIED, "YOU MUST LOVE THE LORD YOUR GOD WITH ALL YOUR HEART, ALL YOUR SOUL, AND ALL YOUR MIND."
>
> MATTHEW 22:36-37 NLT

When you say God's name, He answers, whether you meant to call on Him or not.

YOU CAN DO IT

What can I do? I'm tired of being made fun of! I am fifteen years old. I'm 5 feet, 5 inches tall, and I weigh 250 pounds. My doctor says I'm not healthy, but no matter how hard I try I can't lose weight.

When it comes to weight loss and eating disorders, there are no easy answers. But here are a few things I encourage you to try.

1. Get a complete physical. When you want to lose weight, make sure you do it under the care of a physician. There is no such thing as a quick fix or diet fad that will help you instantly lose weight. If the doctor doesn't find anything physically wrong with you (like a thyroid condition) that's causing weight gain, then with his or her help move to the next step.

2. Choose a healthy weight loss plan. Find a plan that works for you. The best plans will help you learn a new way of eating and exercising and will also provide you with accountability. I have a friend who enrolled in the Weight Watchers program, which challenged him to exercise daily and eat right. He asked me to be his accountability partner. My job was to cheer him on with his victories and help him stay focused after a defeat. Sure, he had some setbacks, but a year later he looks great and feels better than ever. Find an accountability partner to help you through what, at fifteen,

could be one of the most challenging yet victorious times of your life. This person needs to be loving and caring yet brutally honest.

3. Seek counsel. The Bible says, "For lack of guidance a nation falls, but many advisers make victory sure" (Proverbs 11:14). In addition to choosing the right weight loss plan, get counseling to help you understand how you reached this point. A counselor can help you decide if you have a common problem called "compulsive eating disorder," where people try to cope with their problems by eating a lot. And these people really can't overcome their eating disorders until they figure out the causes behind them. A trained counselor can often help them get to the root of their problem, resulting in a more effective way of losing weight.

> **I CAN DO EVERY-
> THING WITH THE
> HELP OF CHRIST
> WHO GIVES ME
> THE STRENGTH I
> NEED.**
>
> **PHILIPPIANS 4:13**
> **NLT**

4. Seek God's help. God created your body, and He can give you the strength to help you overcome your circumstances. My friend who's done so well this past year recently stood up at church and said, "This has been the best year of my life. I want to acknowledge God's presence. I couldn't have done it on my own."

You also won't be able to do it alone. But God doesn't expect you to. Through Christ, He will give you the strength you need.

God is more than enough—whatever your need.

RECOGNIZE HIS VOICE

How can I better listen for God's answers? I really believe in the power of prayer, but I sometimes have trouble listening to God.

In order to hear God, you have to learn to recognize His voice. It's a very important part of our two-way relationship with God. Samuel, an Old Testament prophet, learned this lesson as a young boy. God spoke to him in an audible voice, but Samuel didn't know who was talking to him. Eli, a priest who was older and wiser, helped Samuel determine that he was hearing God's voice. Eli instructed him to respond, "Speak, LORD, for your servant is listening" (1 Samuel 3:9).

Today, God doesn't need to speak in an audible voice. He has given us His Word, the Bible. That's the main way He communicates with us. He also uses people and circumstances. But figuring out what God is trying to say to you isn't easy. Like Samuel, you'll have to learn to recognize God's voice.

Here are a couple of ways you can do this:

1. Make an appointment with God. Spend some time with Him in a quiet place. Read His Word, sing a worship song, praise Him, thank Him, confess your sins to Him, and ask for His presence in your life.

2. Take time to empty your mind. Be quiet before the Lord. Bring a journal and write whatever flows through your mind. Everything

you write down won't be coming from God. But the more time you spend in solitude, the more you'll be able to discipline yourself to listen to God.

Most of us don't take the time to experience silence and solitude. Jesus set an excellent example when he "went off to a solitary place, where he prayed" (Mark 1:35). Jesus recognized listening as a part of praying. His strength came from His solitude.

We often rush through our prayer time, if we ever have it, and then are off doing whatever is next on our busy schedule. Jesus found His strength in listening to His Father. If solitude was necessary for Jesus, it seems like it should be essential for us too.

THE GATEKEEPER OPENS THE GATE FOR HIM, AND THE SHEEP HEAR HIS VOICE. HE CALLS HIS OWN SHEEP BY NAME AND LEADS THEM OUT. WHEN HE HAS BROUGHT OUT ALL HIS OWN, HE GOES AHEAD OF THEM, AND THE SHEEP FOLLOW HIM BECAUSE THEY KNOW HIS VOICE.

JOHN 10:3-4 NRSV

Become familiar with your Heavenly Father's voice and you won't be deceived by a stranger's.

BUILDING CONFIDENT FRIENDS

What can I do? My best friend has really low self-esteem. I've tried to help her, but nothing seems to work. She thinks my other friends and I are lying to her whenever we compliment her.

There's not much you can do or say to change someone's mind about his or her self-image. But you can make a difference by being a caring and supportive friend. When your friend knows you are there for her, regardless of how she feels about herself, her personal outlook can begin to change.

For example, consider Jennifer. She once said: "I hate myself. I'm ugly, I'm stupid, and I can't even imagine that God would love a person like me."

Enter Robin.

Robin stuck by her and, by being a good friend, showed her the love of God. As Jennifer grew and matured, her self-image began to change.

Today Jennifer is one of the key women youth speakers in America. She has often said, "I wouldn't be the person I am today if it weren't for Robin."

God loves us unconditionally, not for what we do but for who we are. God promises that He will never leave us nor forsake us (Hebrews 13:5). When we finally grasp that concept, we can be free to like who we are because we know and believe God's promises. Share this verse with your friend, plus a few others like Genesis 1:31, Psalm 139:13-16, and Ephesians 2:10. The Bible is an excellent resource. Use it to help your friend.

> **GOD CREATED PEOPLE IN HIS OWN IMAGE; GOD PATTERNED THEM AFTER HIMSELF; MALE AND FEMALE HE CREATED THEM.**
>
> **GENESIS 1:27 NLT**

We know we are beautiful; we look like God.

CAUGHT IN THE MIDDLE

My parents recently got divorced. Since the divorce they've each found someone new. They want me to be happy for them and to accept the new people in their lives. I'm not trying to hurt my parents, but I find it difficult to even carry on a conversation with these people because I feel like I'm betraying my other parent. Please help.

One of the most common reactions of kids dealing with divorce is feeling torn between Mom and Dad. When this happens, it's important to remember your parents made the decision to separate—you didn't.

Unfortunately that fact doesn't stop divorce from affecting you. In fact, one consequence is that there may eventually be someone else in the picture. You're in a difficult situation, but I don't think you're betraying either parent by having a conversation with the "other person."

I suggest talking to your parents about your feelings. (If you need to organize your thoughts, write them down first.) Tell your parents you love them. Then tell them you have a hard time talking with their newfound loves because you feel like you're betraying the other parent when you do. Ask them to be patient and understanding as you're also trying to work through the divorce.

In addition to going to God for strength and encouragement, you might also consider seeing a professional Christian counselor to help you sort out your feelings. Talking through your feelings and dealing with your emotions is the first step toward maintaining healthy relationships. More importantly, it will help you begin to heal.

GOD IS OUR REFUGE AND STRENGTH, A VERY PRESENT HELP IN TROUBLE.

PSALM 46:1 NKJV

You can get through it with God on your side.

A MOST IMPORTANT CALL

I'm thirteen and I need my mom as a friend. I can't tell her anything because she doesn't have time for me. I want to be closer to her, but I don't know how. Any advice?

Talk with your mom and tell her how you feel. Try not to make her feel guilty, but instead focus on how you're feeling. Don't shame her into spending time with you, but tell her specifically what you need or want from her. If she's too busy to sit down with you, write her a note. Say something like, "Mom, I love you, and I really want to spend some time with you. I know you're busy, but I would like to invite you to go out to lunch with me this Saturday."

Use this time to talk about your relationship. Your mom can be very special to you during your teenage years, but she can't and shouldn't always be just a friend to you. Sometimes the role of a mom is to show guidance, establish boundaries, and provide discipline. At thirteen, you really do need your mom's relationship. There may be no one besides God who is more important to your growth through the teenage years than your mom. Your mom will thank you for reminding her of her most important calling from God—to be your mom.

Take the initiative and make it happen.

> **BY LOOKING AT [OLDER WOMEN], THE YOUNGER WOMEN WILL KNOW HOW TO LOVE THEIR HUSBANDS AND CHILDREN, BE VIRTUOUS AND PURE, KEEP A GOOD HOUSE, BE GOOD WIVES.**
>
> **TITUS 2:4-5 MSG**

WORK ON THE NEW YOU

How can I change? My reputation is so bad that my pastor and youth pastor have a hard time believing I actually had a deep spiritual conversion. I want to change my life, but it's hard. And it seems that every step I take, I take two steps back. I always get pulled back down. I don't know who to look to for help.

There is an incredibly encouraging story in the Bible about Jesus meeting someone with a bad reputation. In fact, this was a woman who'd been caught in the act of adultery. After she got caught, someone brought her to Jesus and a crowd of people so she could be punished in public. Jewish law said that as her punishment, she had to stand still while others threw stones at her. The stones would keep coming until the woman died.

But Jesus looked out at the crowd and said, "If anyone of you is without sin, let him be the first to throw a stone at her." Everyone dropped the stones they were holding and left. Jesus looked that woman in the eyes and asked her, "Woman, where are [your accusers]? Has no one condemned you?" She answered, "No one, sir."

Then Jesus said something that affects each one of us. With a great deal of compassion and love, Jesus said, "Then neither do I condemn you. Go now and leave your life of sin." This story, from John 8:1-11, is one of the greatest examples of the forgiveness Christ offers us.

I don't know what kind of conversion experience you had, but I hope it involved a real understanding of what it means to follow Christ. Just like the woman in the story, you've been confronted with God's love and mercy, and now you must decide what you'll do about it. You can repent and live for God, or you can continue to make unwise decisions. As you choose the path your life will take, here are a few things to keep in mind:

Change can only come from God. It's a good thing that true change comes from God, not from our own willpower. We are often too weak to change, but God's power combined with your willingness can equal miraculous change. So make sure you stay plugged in to Him through daily prayer, time spent reading the Bible, and fellowship with other Christians.

Change takes accountability and counsel. I find that when I make a decision to change my behavior, it helps to tell someone about my decision. Talk with your pastor, youth pastor, or a spiritual leader in your life and tell him or her about your desire to grow spiritually. Ask if you can check in with him or her at least once a week and talk honestly about your successes as well as your struggles. It can be a weekly phone call or even a thirty-second conversation at church. Even though your pastors are having a hard time taking your conversion seriously, they may change their minds if you're sincere about wanting to change and you show them you're willing to work at it.

Change takes discipline. I like the advice the apostle Paul gave to his disciple Timothy when he said, "Train yourself to be godly" (1 Timothy 4:7). As you develop the basic practices of your faith (prayer, Bible reading, fellowship), you'll see the reversal of your "one step forward and two steps back" pattern. Pretty soon I think you'll find yourself making a habit of living in a way that honors God.

True change comes from God, not from our own willpower.

THEREFORE, IF ANYONE IS IN CHRIST, HE IS A NEW CREATION; THE OLD HAS GONE, THE NEW HAS COME!

2 CORINTHIANS 5:17

LOOK FOR WHAT'S RIGHT

How can my brother and I get past our differences and learn to get along? My brother is a year younger than I, and we fight all the time. We both go to church and attend our youth group, but he's not interested in really living for Christ. He uses bad language and listens to a lot of raunchy music. We used to have a great brother/sister relationship, and I'd like to have that again.

Restoring your relationship is going to take patience, understanding, and a lot of commitment on your part. With that in mind, there are a few things you need to remember.

First, think about other relationships in your life. I'll bet each of them has had ups and downs. Even best friends argue, disagree, and think differently about important issues. But when you are committed to a friendship, you're willing to work through those differences and repair the friendship. The same is true in your relationship with your brother. So don't let yourself get too worried that the way things are right now is the way they will be forever.

Also, realize your brother may be going through a rebellious stage in his life. But no matter how he acts on the outside, he most likely still needs to feel loved and cared for. By sticking by him and continuing to show him you care, you'll send an invaluable message to your brother—one that says your love is permanent and unconditional.

To show your brother that kind of love, you need to focus on what's right in your relationship. Think about some of the things you have in common. Do you both like sports? Is there a movie or TV show that always makes you two laugh? Anything that helps you stay connected with your brother can help get you through this tough time.

HE HAS GIVEN US THIS COMMAND: WHOEVER LOVES GOD MUST ALSO LOVE HIS BROTHER.

1 JOHN 4:21

Even if you can't find any common interests, you can still connect with your brother by expressing interest in his life. Yes, he's listening to music you find offensive, but do your best not to judge your brother. If you really want to be close to him again, you won't get very far by criticizing him or pointing out all the ways he's messing up. Instead, continue to show your brother God's love through your patience and care.

Finally, watch out for your brother. His change in behavior may indicate other, more dangerous changes, like alcohol or drug use. You don't need to spy on him, but be aware of who he's hanging out with and what kind of things he's doing after school. If you become concerned about anything, talk to your parents or another trusted adult, like your youth pastor.

Most importantly, pray for your brother. Ask God to be with him and to guide his decisions. And ask for God's wisdom as you work to repair your relationship.

After all of this, remember that your brother may not respond the way you want him to. But be patient. Hopefully, he will move out of this phase. My guess is that he really does want to be close to you too, but he may not know how.

I know a brother and sister who are very close. They are each married and have their own families now, but even their families are the best of friends. They told me it wasn't always this way. After I read your letter, I called them and asked their advice. I think their answer is worth repeating: "Even in the most difficult times, try not to do permanent damage to the relationship and don't give up. A brother/sister relationship is a lifelong relationship, and when your brother gets through this awkward stage he will again look to your relationship as a priority."

Encouragement empowers a relationship.

BEAUTY THAT TOUCHES OTHERS

How can I feel better about myself? I've spent many years hating myself because of my looks. People call me "fat" and "ugly." I've tried new hairstyles, makeup, and new clothes, but nothing seems to help. I hate feeling sorry for myself, but I can't help it. It really hurts when people call me names. I'm a caring, loving person, and I know God loves me; but I still feel so depressed about my looks.

As I read your letter, I wished so badly that we could meet face-to-face and I could just give you a friendly hug. You sound like a fine person—a person who deserves to be reminded she's worth caring about.

I want to tell you a story about a woman I know who once felt much like you do. I hope her story will help you stay focused on the kind of beauty that's truly important.

Sydney was one of those people who had a great personality, but I'll be honest, many people felt she wasn't very attractive. I know Sydney tried to lose weight, and I know she was hurt that she didn't get asked on dates. She had a hard time convincing herself that she was a good and lovable person.

But despite her struggles to feel good about herself, Sydney made some very good decisions along the way. She stayed close to God. She worked hard to develop good friendships with guys. She joined a prayer group at church, and she was always one of the first to volunteer to serve when there was a need.

She may not have been the most attractive girl on the outside, but as she grew in her faith and learned more about giving to others, she became radiant on the inside. This doesn't mean she didn't struggle with her self-image, but she kept working on it.

I remember a Scripture passage that was important to Sydney. It was part of a conversation the Lord had with the prophet Samuel about a good-looking person who lacked inner beauty:

"But the LORD said to Samuel, 'Do not consider his appearance or his height, for I have rejected him. The LORD does not look at the things man looks at. Man looks at the outward appearance, but the LORD looks at the heart'" (1 Samuel 16:7).

Today, Sydney is happily married with two beautiful children. Sydney teaches Sunday school for the youth group at her church, and the students absolutely love her. Whenever she tells her students about her difficult high

> YOU FORMED MY INWARD PARTS; YOU WOVE ME IN MY MOTHER'S WOMB. I WILL GIVE THANKS TO YOU, FOR I AM FEARFULLY AND WONDERFULLY MADE; WONDERFUL ARE YOUR WORKS, AND MY SOUL KNOWS IT VERY WELL. MY FRAME WAS NOT HIDDEN FROM YOU, WHEN I WAS MADE IN SECRET, {AND} SKILLFULLY WROUGHT IN THE DEPTHS OF THE EARTH; YOUR EYES HAVE SEEN MY UNFORMED SUBSTANCE; AND IN YOUR BOOK WERE ALL WRITTEN THE DAYS THAT WERE ORDAINED {FOR ME,} WHEN AS YET THERE WAS NOT ONE OF THEM.
>
> PSALM 139:13-16
> NASB

school days, they can hardly believe it. She is one of their heroes. And you know what? Although she will never be considered physically beautiful, her inner beauty overflows, making her a very attractive woman on the inside and the outside.

I hope you will follow Sydney's example. Stay faithful to God. Surround yourself with positive Christian friends. When you're hurting, be sure and share your pain with these friends. And find ways to reach out and serve others. If you concentrate on being beautiful to God, your inner beauty will touch everyone you meet.

Remember who created you.

KEEP THE FIRE BURNING

How can I keep the excitement for God I had at camp? I spent a week at a Bible camp this summer and had a blast! But now I'm home, and I just don't feel like I can keep my faith strong without my camp friends.

It's easy to get excited about God and feel unbelievably close to Him at camp. When you mix the intense times with God with a whole lot of fun, you get a lifelong, positive memory. And that's why a lot of people find it hard to come down off that camp "high."

By its very design, camp is a "mountaintop experience." It's meant to be a time to jump-start your faith. The hard part is what you're experiencing now, the letdown. But the good news is that you can use what you learned during your time at camp to make your "real life" faith much stronger. I've found a way to help myself make the most of life's "mountaintop experiences." This formula helps me feel close to God, even when I've come down off that mountain. I call it the GROW plan:

Go to God daily in prayer. Most likely you prayed often at camp, so keep up the habit with a daily quiet time with God (1 Thessalonians 5:17).

Read the Bible often. God's Word will reveal much of His will for your life, and it will keep your faith strong.

Obey God's Word. As you obey the Lord, you will know His presence and keep from making unwise decisions (John 14:21).

OUR GOD [IS INDEED] A CONSUMING FIRE.

HEBREWS 12:29 AMP

Worship and serve God with other believers. Just like at camp, fellowship with other Christians is often what carries us through the hard times and encourages us to stay firm in our faith (Psalm 150:6, Hebrews 10:24-25).

I can't promise you'll always have the same awesome feelings you had at camp, but if you follow the GROW plan, you'll develop strong faith.

Grow a faith that can carry you through life's valleys and up to the next mountaintop.

TAKE OWNERSHIP

The church I go to believes dancing is wrong. That hasn't been a big deal to me until this year. I'm a junior, and we have the Junior Ball coming up. I know there will be dancing there, but I really want to go. What should I do?

What you end up doing—whether you go to the dance or not—isn't as important as the questions you work through to reach your decision. The questions you're probably already asking yourself are, "Why is dancing wrong?" and "If I go to the ball, what will people at my church say?"

Now is the best time to begin taking ownership of your beliefs. But you should also get together with your parents and your youth leader or pastor to discuss this further. Is your church really dead set against dancing, or only certain kinds of dancing? What is the biblical basis for this belief? See if they might have some practical guidelines for you if you go to the ball. And ask them, "What advice would you give me in seeking God's direction in dancing and other cultural issues?"

You might be pleasantly surprised by what you hear. On the other hand, you may find your parents also have reservations about dancing. If they're not open to further discussion, I think you should respect their wishes by planning an alternate event or staying home.

Let's say you don't get a strong response either way. This is your chance to ask God for wisdom as you make a decision.

Take ownership of your beliefs by using wisdom in the choices you make.

IF YOU NEED WISDOM—IF YOU WANT TO KNOW WHAT GOD WANTS YOU TO DO—ASK HIM, AND HE WILL GLADLY TELL YOU. HE WILL NOT RESENT YOUR ASKING.

JAMES 1:5 NLT

REALISTIC EXPECTATIONS

I really want a close relationship with my dad, but it's difficult—isn't that what God would want? Until about a year and a half ago, I lived with my mom. Now I'm living with my dad, whom I haven't lived with in ten years. He's an alcoholic, and he doesn't like my Christian beliefs. He'll call home when he's drunk and swear and insult me. He's consumed with his job, his girlfriend, and alcohol. I dread seeing him. What can I do?

You've already done something significant by acknowledging that your dad is an alcoholic. He's addicted to a mood- and mind-altering drug, and you suffer the consequences of that addiction.

As you well know, living with an alcoholic isn't easy. I know, too—I grew up with alcoholism in my family. But it might help you to know that your dad probably doesn't like living with himself, either. He knows his alcoholism is partly to blame for some of the severe problems your family faces. Quite possibly he's tried to quit drinking at one time or another, but because of his intense addiction, and because alcohol effectively medicates his pain and relieves stress, he's been unsuccessful.

Let me give you four pieces of advice. First, begin meeting with someone who knows about being the child of an alcoholic. You can receive needed information and support from others who have struggled with the same situation. A school counselor can help you find this vital help. I would also recommend looking in the local phone book for Alateen and Al-Anon support groups (or call 888-425-2666 for a local chapter).

> **YOU ARE MY HIDING PLACE AND MY SHIELD; I HOPE IN YOUR WORD.**
>
> **PSALM 119:114**
>
> **NKJV**

Second, continue communicating with your dad. Once you start receiving outside support, you'll gain more confidence to talk with your dad about your desire for a meaningful, deeper relationship. Tell your dad you love him. But remember: most alcoholics have a difficult time with intimacy.

You might have to lower your expectations of a "perfect" home and relationship. As you seek a healthier relationship, don't be afraid to call your dad's problem by name. He's an alcoholic; tell him you believe he can get help for his alcoholism. You can even help him find a local chapter of Alcoholics Anonymous by checking the phone book or going to www.alcoholics-anonymous.org.

Third, don't neglect yourself and your own needs. There is always the temptation to feel like you're responsible for somehow "fixing" your dad. You're not. You are responsible for taking care of yourself, so be sure you do. Build good friendships. Get exercise. Eat healthy. Find ways to relax and simply enjoy life. And be sure you stay away from alcohol and other substances. As strange as it sounds, children of alcoholics often turn to alcohol or other drugs to solve their problems. Don't give in to the temptation.

Finally, don't neglect your spiritual life. I like these verses: "You, Lord, give true peace to those who depend on you, because they trust you. So, trust the Lord always, because he is our Rock forever"

(Isaiah 26:3-4, NCV). God doesn't promise us an easy life, but He does promise to walk with us through our times of trouble.

As a Christian growing up in a family crippled by alcoholism, I felt at times like my faith was misunderstood. I wanted the kind of relationship with my parents that you want with your dad. And to be honest, I eventually gave up much hope in the situation ever changing. The fervent prayers I prayed in high school became less regular.

But God did get ahold of my family. It wasn't while I was still in high school, but today we have the relationship I always longed for. Keep praying for your dad, and don't give up hope.

Expect God to come through for you in a way that is bigger than you are.

GOD³

Why do we call God "Father"? And what role does the Father have in our lives that's different from Jesus and the Holy Spirit?

To answer your first question, we call God "Father" because Jesus said to. He instructed His disciples to pray to "Abba" (Matthew 6:5-15), which means "Daddy" in English. Never before had God, the almighty creator of the universe, been addressed so personally and informally in prayer. With just one word, Jesus showed that God is our loving Father and we are His children.

Now about the role of the Father. Your question deals with one of the great doctrines of Christianity called the Trinity. Although it's a very difficult idea to grasp, we believe in one God in three persons: the Father, the Son (Jesus), and the Holy Spirit. Each person of the Trinity has a distinct role. Generally speaking, God the Father is the Creator, Jesus is our Savior, and the Holy Spirit lives in each Christian, comforting, empowering, and leading. But even that's an oversimplification; in reality, the roles are shared by all three persons of the Trinity. The Trinity is a complex concept, and even the world's top theologians have difficulty defining the roles of all three persons.

But it's not important to have the Trinity all figured out. What's important is worshiping and loving the great God the Trinity represents.

Think of the Trinity as God to the third power.

"GO THEREFORE AND MAKE
DISCIPLES OF ALL NATIONS,
BAPTIZING THEM IN THE NAME OF
THE FATHER AND OF THE SON AND
OF THE HOLY SPIRIT, AND
TEACHING THEM TO OBEY
EVERYTHING THAT I HAVE
COMMANDED YOU. AND REMEMBER,
I AM WITH YOU ALWAYS, TO THE
END OF THE AGE."

MATTHEW 28:19-20 NRSV

IT TAKES GRACE

What can I do? A few months ago, I found out my best friend was stealing. Not just from stores, but from my friends and me too. My friends and I told her how we felt. She seemed really sorry, and for a while she stopped. Then, just a few days ago, she confessed that she'd stolen a shirt from me a few weeks earlier. I think she's a kleptomaniac. I've prayed and talked to her about it, but I can't trust her anymore. We've been friends since first grade, and I don't want to lose her as my friend.

There are several reasons why your friend may be stealing. Authorities on the subject say compulsive stealing is often a result of a person's poor self-image. It sounds like your friend definitely has a serious problem that's larger than anything you can fix on your own. Your friend needs the help of a professional Christian counselor who can help her overcome her compulsion to steal. With that in mind, I want to focus on your concerns about keeping her as a friend.

Yes, she has a problem. But the fact that she was honest enough to admit that she stole from you offers a little bit of hope for both of you. She obviously wants to keep your friendship. And for now, that's enough to go on.

This may sound crazy, but I don't think you have to trust her to remain her friend. Sure, there must be some basic trust, but you don't have to give her your full trust. You can show her care and friendship even though you don't have complete trust in her. In some ways, this will be a one-sided friendship. You may end up doing more giving than getting for a while. Until she gets help and stops stealing, you can fill your need for trustworthy friends in other relationships.

She clearly trusts you. She knows you're the kind of friend she needs to help her get over this problem. If she didn't feel that way, I doubt she'd have listened to the concerns you and your other friends expressed. I doubt she would have told you about stealing your shirt. And I doubt she'd still be interested in having any kind of friendship with you. So she wants to hold on to your friendship.

With this in mind, I encourage you to tell her that trust is an important part of a healthy friendship, the kind you want with her. Tell her how much you care about her and that you value the friend-ship you share. Let her know that her efforts to be honest about her problem are good steps toward earning your trust.

No one is perfect, so assure her that's not what you expect from her. But help her see that her stealing is unacceptable. Encourage her to keep on working to overcome this obvious problem in her life. If she's open to seeking the professional help she needs, do what you can to help her find it. Offer to pray with her, and let her know you're praying for her on your own. Help her build other solid friendships with Christians who can do the same.

There is a pretty incredible story in the Bible about a time Jesus encountered a woman who was caught in the act of adultery. The people wanted to kill her because that was what the Old Testament told them they could do. But Jesus taught a new way of doing things. He looked out at the woman's accusers and said, "If any one of you is without sin, let him be the first to throw a stone at her."

When the people in the crowd heard these words, they dropped their stones and went away. Jesus then had a deeply personal conversation with the woman. He said to her, "Woman, where are they? Has no one condemned you?" She replied, "No one, sir." Then Jesus looked her in the eye with love and compassion and said, "Then neither do I condemn you. Now go and leave your life of sin." (You can find this story in John 8:3-11.)

> **HE WHO LOVES PURITY AND THE PURE IN HEART AND WHO IS GRACIOUS IN SPEECH—BECAUSE OF THE GRACE OF HIS LIPS WILL HE HAVE THE KING FOR HIS FRIEND.**
>
> **PROVERBS 22:11 AMP**

Jesus is a good model for how you can deal with your friend. Jesus didn't approve of the adulterous woman's sin. He didn't just ignore her sin. He told her in strong words to stop sinning. But He also chose to not condemn her, even though He had every reason to.

You have plenty of reasons to end your friendship with this girl, but it sounds like you want to keep it. Good for you. You don't have to tolerate your friend's stealing, but you can show her compassion. Hang in there with your friend, if you can, and you may just help her change her lifestyle of stealing. The combination of God's help, possibly the help of a professional, and your friendship may be the keys for your friend to choose the better road.

Experiencing true grace can help a friend get rid of the sin in his or her life.

EMOTIONAL REPAIR

After my boyfriend and I broke up we became friends, but lately we have gotten in fights. I have tried to apologize and be nice, but he is always very rude and mean to me.

What you are describing is very common. Once a couple begins to date there is a new intimacy between them. They have crossed the line of friendship and entered the world of exclusive dating. And dating, in fact, is a type of practice toward marriage.

Then, when a couple breaks up, it becomes very difficult to reestablish the former friendship. In fact, many cannot go back to being just friends. It's impossible to walk backward on the path of intimacy, even if the intimacy developed was only holding hands.

I would encourage you to give him some space and not expect too much on the subject of friendship. Continue to be polite, and do not speak negatively of him to your friends. If he will not accept your apology, that is his choice. You must do your best to do what is right, but you cannot make someone else do anything. How he chooses to respond to you is his choice.

It is likely that in the future you will regain your friendship with him. For now, allow some space between the two of you. Focus on your relationship with God, your family, and your girlfriends. Enjoy your time in high school and the life God has given you. There's plenty of time later to be involved in dating relationships.

Focus on your relationship with God.

THE PERSON WHO LIVES IN RIGHT
RELATIONSHIP WITH GOD DOES IT
BY EMBRACING WHAT GOD
ARRANGES FOR HIM.

GALATIANS 3:11 MSG

PURITY—IT'S YOUR CHOICE

Have I gone past the point of God being able to forgive me? I have become sexually active with my current boyfriend. I have been raised in a Christian home, and I know that sex before marriage is wrong. The only thing is that we haven't had sexual intercourse. Am I still a virgin? I have repented and asked God's forgiveness many times over for what we have done, but I still stumble.

The first thing to remember is that God loves you and is ready to forgive you for anything, anytime! He does desire that we don't just sit back and keep going on in the same direction, but that we repent and seek purity and what God would want in our relationships.

As for your question about your virginity, losing our virginity comes only when we have sexual intercourse with another person. Therefore, you are still a virgin. The question though is what course are you heading down. Most likely, if you keep on this course you will end up losing your virginity.

If you are serious about going in a new direction, there are a few things that you need to keep in mind.

• Make a decision as a couple to stop being sexually active.

- Set some boundaries. Find out what leads you to be sexually active and make a decision to keep yourselves out of those situations.

- Remember that it is only through God's power, not our might, that we can keep going in the right direction. Pray together and seek God as a couple.

- Seek accountability. Find others who you will be completely honest and transparent with. Allow those people to ask anything at anytime. If you are tempted, call them and seek support from them.

Purity is one of the most important things you can seek. It's hard, but well worth the effort!

IT IS GOD'S WILL THAT YOU SHOULD BE SANCTIFIED: THAT YOU SHOULD AVOID SEXUAL IMMORALITY; THAT EACH OF YOU SHOULD LEARN TO CONTROL HIS OWN BODY IN A WAY THAT IS HOLY AND HONORABLE.

1 THESSOLONIANS 4:3-4

RESPECT ONE ANOTHER

I have two Christian friends who have been dating for about a year. The guy is going to buy a house next year, and his girlfriend is going to live with him. They will have a house to themselves. Does it say in the Bible how far you should go with a person, or if this type of thing is permitted? I'm unsure. I believe it is wrong, but I can't just say my personal opinion. I would love biblical advice and advice from older Christians to help them with this issue.

I don't think it is a good idea for an unmarried couple to live together.

As a starting point, let me say that God created sex to be expressed within the marriage relationship. See Matthew 19:4-6, Hebrews 13:4, 1 Corinthians 6:18-20.

In regard to your friends' potential situation, there is no Bible passage which says that unmarried people aren't supposed to live together in the same house before marriage. Yet, with our starting point that sex is designed for the marriage relationship, it would be very difficult for the average couple not to be tempted sexually while living together. God calls us to respect each other, do what is best for one another, and maintain purity (Philippians 2:3-5 and 1 Thessalonians 4:3-8).

On a completely common-sense level, living together (and being sexually active) with no marriage commitment to one another can lead to a lot of heartache down the road for either person.

When speaking with your friends about your beliefs, be gentle and loving. Don't use the Scriptures as a weapon to hit your friends with. "A gentle answer turns away wrath, but a harsh word stirs up anger" (Proverbs 15:1). They might very well be struggling over what the right thing to do might be. Don't reject them, but walk alongside them during this process.

> **"IF YOU LOVE ME, OBEY MY COMMAND-MENTS."**
>
> **JOHN 14:15 NLT**

Finally, there are some other questions and answers on our Web site, www.youthbuilders.com, that I think might help you address this issue with your friends. Do a search of our questions and answers using the word "sex."

Our proof in our commitment to God is in our sincere determination to obey Him.

HONOR GOD IN ALL THINGS

I have been dating the same guy for over three years. We've broken up a lot because I wanted to pursue only God, and our relationship wasn't glorifying to the Lord. But I've always had a boyfriend, so when we'd break up, I'd find my value in and spend my time with another boy—never focusing on the Lord.

I love my boyfriend, and though he pushes me to change myself to become what God wants me to, he thinks our physical relationship is okay. Often I do too. I try to justify it. I want desperately to get out of the relationship, but I have no good reason to tell him. I've never lived up to what I say I'll do. He's been faithful and chased me and loves me, but I don't know what's best for me. I can pursue God when we're together, but I hate myself for compromising my convictions on sexual things.

It sounds like you already know the right thing to do and that you are just needing some confirmation. Well, here it is. You are right that God wants a deep and personal relationship with you and that it takes time to pursue that. You also rightly identify your need to find your worth in God and not in a relationship with anyone else. God created you and is pleased with you regardless of what you do or who you are with. And, since you are His child, He has some standards that have been put in place to protect you.

Sexual activity prior to marriage is almost always a relationship killer. Statistics show that when a couple engages in premarital sexual activity, they have a higher rate of divorce as well as sexual problems within marriage. If your boyfriend really loves you like he says, he will put your needs in front of his own and gladly wait for marriage to enjoy the privilege of a sexual relationship.

I am going to challenge your idea that you can pursue God when you are in a relationship that is opposite to the will of God. I find nowhere in Scripture that God blesses sin or the relationship surrounding the sin. The reason you say you hate yourself for compromising your convictions is that you know the right thing to do, and the Holy Spirit is convicting you.

I also disagree that you have no good reason to get out of the relationship. Some of the reasons include:

1. It is not God-honoring.

2. You are not happy.

4. Your boyfriend is pushing you to compromise your faith and give in to sin.

5. You are very young to have already been in a three-year relationship.

6. The relationship is hindering your walk with God.

You have some decisions you must make.

1. Are you going to pursue this relationship? If so, what boundaries will you put in place to make sure you remain abstinent from now until marriage?

2. Are you willing to break off this relationship if your boyfriend does not agree to your decision to remain abstinent until marriage?

The most important relationship you will ever have is your relationship with God. I encourage you to regain that relationship and allow God to pour out His healing love over you so that you find your worth only in Christ and do not seek your worth from any other relationship.

It sounds like you need some time to heal. I strongly encourage you to take that time. If needed, seek some help from a professional Christian counselor (preferably female). You have the rest of your life ahead of you. Care for yourself, seek the heart and healing of God, and have the courage to change.

IF YOUR LIFE HONORS THE NAME OF JESUS, HE WILL HONOR YOU. GRACE IS BEHIND AND THROUGH ALL OF THIS, OUR GOD GIVING HIMSELF FREELY, THE MASTER, JESUS CHRIST, GIVING HIMSELF FREELY.

2 THESSALONIANS 1:12 MSG

May God give you wisdom and strength as you pursue a path of change.

A CHOICE TO FOLLOW

Can you help me understand this? My mom is a lesbian. I know that the Bible says it is wrong, but my mom says she falls in love with a person because of who the person is inside. So my mom feels like it's OK if the person she loves is a woman. Why would God condemn my mom when she's trying to love people for who they are? I really worry she is going to go to hell.

Let me start by clearly saying this: God loves your mom. God allowed His only Son, Jesus, to die for all people—including your mom.

Homosexuality is a very complicated and disturbing sin to many people, partially because they can't understand it. That may explain why some people act and talk as though homosexuality is a worse sin than others. Some people may not like what I'm going to say, but I don't think your mother's sin of homosexuality is any worse than that of the guy I know from my church who committed adultery or the teenage girl who lies to her parents. In fact, there are references to all kinds of sin throughout the Bible, and only a few relate directly to homosexuality.

In Greek, the original language of the New Testament, the word "sin" literally means "to miss the mark." You don't get any extra points for missing by only a few inches. And you don't rack up penalty points for missing by a mile. You either hit the mark, or you don't. And we all miss the mark—I do, you do, and your mom does.

I also believe the Bible is the Word of God, and I do believe the Bible clearly states that homosexuality is a sin. Your mom might disagree with me, but I have to stand by the authority of Scripture.

Still, my main concern right now is not so much your mom's sexual preference as it is her relationship with Jesus Christ. If she truly gives her life to Christ, confesses her sin (not just sexual sin, but all sin), and accepts His death on the cross as God's ultimate act of forgiveness, then she will be saved. Romans 10:9-10 says, "If you confess with your mouth, 'Jesus is Lord,' and believe in your heart that God raised him from the dead, you will be saved. For it is with your heart that you believe and are justified, and it is with your mouth that you confess and are saved." It doesn't matter if you're a homosexual, a liar, a cheat, or any other kind of sinner; the way to salvation is the same for everyone.

If people make a sincere profession of faith in Christ according to Romans 10:9-10, they will want to make Jesus the Lord of their lives, and they will look to the authority of the Bible for guidance. They will desire to live a life free from sin. They will strive to glorify God in all they say and do. For some people, that might mean they give up a way of life based on greed and deceit. For others, it might mean they no longer lie or gossip about others.

For a homosexual, it means seeking a lifestyle that is consistent with the Bible's views on sexuality. Of course, no one can ever live completely free from sin, but following Christ means we do everything in our power to honor God with the way we live.

I think it's safe to say God is less concerned with the specific sin in a person's life than with the way sin affects that person. God wants to have a relationship with us, and sin gets in the way. Sin hurts us and makes our lives less than what God wants them to be.

> **"IF ANYONE WISHES TO COME AFTER ME, HE MUST DENY HIMSELF, AND TAKE UP HIS CROSS AND FOLLOW ME."**
>
> **MATTHEW 16:24 NASB**

If your mom is like most homosexuals, I doubt she has lived an easy life. Studies tell us that homosexuals as a group are less happy, less fulfilled, more involved in drug and alcohol abuse, and frankly, often die much earlier than heterosexuals.

So is your mom condemned to hell? I honestly can't answer that question. Ultimately, that's between her and God. If she gives her life to Christ and truly seeks to live for Him, then the Bible promises she'll spend eternity in Heaven. God really does want to know her and see her in Heaven one day (see 2 Peter 3:9). It's up to her to make the choice.

I encourage you to pray for your mom. When you have questions or concerns about your mom's homosexuality, talk to a trustworthy adult from your church. Continue to show your mom love and respect, and let her know you care about her, no matter what.

Following Christ means we do everything in our power to honor God with the way we live.

BIBLICAL CONFRONTATION

What can we do? Our youth director is young, married, and incredibly good-looking. But he's making a lot of people in our youth group very uncomfortable. He's always hugging the girls. He dresses in a sexy way, wearing cut-off T-shirts and ripped jeans with his underwear showing. I'm afraid to be alone with him.

And the guys in our group think he's way too competitive in games. They say he's rough and gets really mad when he loses. My mom talked to him about his behavior, but he laughed off her concerns, saying girls always fantasize about their youth directors. The church committee that works with him just lets him do what he wants. Even worse, the senior pastor is his uncle, so he probably wouldn't do anything either. Most of us love our youth group, but our youth leader is making it miserable.

I believe youth workers have one of God's most important callings. Most of them are committed to sharing God's love with students. But as with any profession, there are a few youth workers who are misguided when it comes to lifestyle choices and appropriate behavior. It's clear your youth director must be confronted with these issues.

Even if just one young woman feels uncomfortable with him, or if only a couple of the guys say he is too rough and competitive, it's time to get the issues on the table and talk. It sounds like you've tried to do just that. I want to encourage you to keep trying, for the good of everyone involved.

I suggest you use the Bible's model for handling conflict, Matthew 18:15-17.

• Write down all the information you know to be fact. Leave out any rumors and anything you can't back up as absolute truth. Talk over this list with your mom, or the adult you plan to take with you in step two.

• Ask your mother or another friend and her parent to go with you to talk to your youth director privately. Confront him with the facts you've gathered. To confront doesn't mean to be negative or critical, but rather tell him in a caring way that you have some concerns about the youth group. If he listens to your concerns and makes some changes in his behavior, stop there and be thankful you've helped.

• If he doesn't take you seriously, bring your concerns to the leadership of your church. This could be a meeting with the pastor, the committee you mentioned, or other leaders in your congregation. Don't assume you know how they will respond. They most likely want what's best for the church and will listen seriously to your concerns.

• Again, stick with the facts. Ask the leadership to hear you, to pray about the next move, and to inform you of what actions they plan to take. Hopefully, your youth director will listen to the leadership and make the necessary changes.

• If nothing changes, you have some difficult decisions to make. The youth group members and their parents could call for a church meeting. You could make an appointment with a representative from your denomination. (The church office can help you find out who that is.) Or you can consider worshiping in another church. These are all very serious steps, and I hope you don't have to take the problem this far.

Your efforts to resolve the problems with your youth director may be just as important for his growth as they are for the group. Remember to pray for him and share your concerns in true Christian love.

Tell the truth with love.

TRULY I TELL YOU, WHATEVER YOU FORBID AND DECLARE TO BE IMPROPER AND UNLAWFUL ON EARTH MUST BE WHAT IS ALREADY FORBIDDEN IN HEAVEN, AND WHATEVER YOU PERMIT AND DECLARE PROPER AND LAWFUL ON EARTH MUST BE WHAT IS ALREADY PERMITTED IN HEAVEN.

MATTHEW 18:18 AMP

YOUR HEART SPEAKS

How can I stop what little swearing I do? I am also trying to be nicer to people. I am usually really nice, but I have a tendency to get angry easily at my boyfriend for things that aren't important. It's not even that he and I are fighting but more like I am trying to pick a fight with him.

First of all, praise God that you are even asking the question and seeking answers for this habit. One of the things I've learned from the Bible is that Jesus said, "What comes out of the mouth starts in our hearts."

What that taught me (I struggled with the same thing when I was a high school student) was that I needed to look at the reason or origin of my language habits. I asked myself some things you could ask yourself: *Am I angry about some things? Am I bitter? Do I have some unresolved personal conflict inside that just comes out of my mouth?* I learned that if I had garbage in my heart, it was going to come out in my speech.

Secondly, get an accountability partner. Tell that person what you want to do and have them help you with your language. Ask your accountability partner to challenge you when you make mistakes (which you will). Don't expect everything to change overnight but give the Holy Spirit time to do His work.

Last and most important, pray! Ask God to transform your heart and your language. If you get in a situation where you are tempted to use bad language, stop and ask yourself what would be appropriate to say under the circumstances.

Also ask yourself, *If Jesus were listening to my conversation, what would He say about it?* Oh, one more thing, sometimes language issues stem from a desire within us to "power up" on people by using language. We lie to ourselves and tell ourselves that "big bad words" are going to communicate to the world that "I am a big, bad person not to be messed with." Lay that before the Lord and one trusted friend as well. God bless you in this incredible spiritual step you are taking!

> **OUT OF THE FULLNESS (THE OVERFLOW, THE SUPERABUNDANCE) OF THE HEART THE MOUTH SPEAKS.**
>
> **MATTHEW 12:34 AMP**

What's in your heart comes out of your mouth. Fill it with the good things of God.

PRIORITIES CHECKLIST

I'm too busy for God! I know that sounds bad, but it's true. I take AP classes and am involved in many extracurricular activities. These things are important to me, and they're important to my future. Does God really want me to give these things up to follow Him?

I don't think God is asking a bright, enthusiastic person like yourself to quit all activities and live like a hermit. However, your first sentence, "I'm too busy for God!" does say a lot about your time commitments and priorities.

You're correct to say that things like AP classes are important to your future; when it comes time to apply to college, you'll have a good chance of being accepted at a number of fine schools. You've clearly invested a great deal of time and energy in preparing for your future, and I hope it pays off. But here's my question to you: Isn't your relationship with God also important to you and your future?

Busy people have always needed to think about their priorities. Jesus asked people to do just that with this powerful statement: "Seek first his kingdom and his righteousness, and all these things will be given to you as well" (Matthew 6:33). In other words, Jesus is asking us to put God first and then watch as everything else falls into place. Putting God first doesn't necessarily mean giving up all your extracurricular activities and AP classes. But it does mean you need to reprioritize your life, keeping your relationship with Christ #1.

Of course, you may find you just can't make God your top priority and still be heavily involved in all these other things. If that's the case, then I think it's time for you to pare down your involvement in extracurricular activities. I'm not saying you have to drop everything, but you may need to end one or two of your commitments.

To do that, make a list of everything you're involved in. Then, look at the list and rank the activities by how much you enjoy them and how well they're preparing you for the future. You might find that there are a few things you can get rid of without cutting back on your favorite activities.

You might also be surprised to know that most colleges are less impressed with the number of extracurricular activities than they are with your level of involvement in those activities. In other words, digging deep into the activities you really love is better than spreading yourself thin across every club, team, and group you can find. Knowing this could help you decide which extracurricular activities you really want to stick with and which ones you're involved in halfheartedly.

> **WHATEVER YOU DO, WHETHER IN WORD OR DEED, DO IT ALL IN THE NAME OF THE LORD JESUS, GIVING THANKS TO GOD THE FATHER THROUGH HIM.**
>
> **COLOSSIANS 3:17**

I'm not sure God wants you to give up some things for Him as much as He wants you to give those things to Him. There is nothing more exciting than people putting God first in their lives and using all their talents for Him. That's why I hope you use your God-given abilities to the glory of God.

Put God first and then watch everything else fall into place.

A MATTER OF HEART

Do you think someone has the right to say one religion is better than others? I believe in God, and I love Him very much. But I think that no one has the right to say whether God exists or doesn't. I don't think people should say their religion is the best. No one should push others to join their religion, and none of us has ever seen God.

Discussions on religion and politics always cause arguments. Just this week, I saw a television news show with a Christian debating a non-Christian about religion and politics. Even though I agreed with the Christian about salvation through Jesus, the authority of the Bible, and his stand on morals and values, I was embarrassed by his mean-spirited behavior to the non-Christian. He was disrespectful and didn't listen to her beliefs.

On the other hand, I have no problem with Christians sharing their faith and talking about their beliefs and experiences with the Lord. Honest dialogue is not offensive, but obnoxious behavior is insulting and hateful. The important thing is the way we communicate our beliefs.

Jesus made some very strong statements. He said, "I am the way and the truth and the life. No one comes to the Father except through me" (John 14:6). Jesus wasn't afraid to articulate what He believed, yet He always did it in love. If you are a Christian, you will have strong beliefs about who God is and many other topics of faith. As a result, some people will think you are close-minded. Still, it is possible to state what you believe and have experienced while at the same time showing love and respect to those who disagree. (For more information, read the first chapter of John.)

You say that no one has ever seen God. But did you know that the Bible teaches that Jesus Christ is the visible image of the invisible God?

And since Jesus is God, His death and resurrection really mean something! God, in His Son, died for our sins. And His resurrection proved He had truly conquered death. What a great and wonderful thing!

I am honored and humbled that Jesus died for my sins and for the world. I often want to share this most incredible news with friends who haven't heard—and it's possible to share the truth in love. I would urge you to read through the Gospels: Matthew, Mark, Luke, and John. Underline the words of Jesus. They are often strong and compassionate at the same time. Jesus didn't compromise His belief, but He was always respectful. He didn't believe that all religions were the same, yet He loved even those who chose to go another way.

> **HE IS THE IMAGE OF THE INVISIBLE GOD, THE FIRSTBORN OF ALL CREATION. FOR BY HIM ALL THINGS WERE CREATED, BOTH IN THE HEAVENS AND ON EARTH, VISIBLE AND INVISIBLE, WHETHER THRONES OR DOMINIONS OR RULERS OR AUTHORITIES— ALL THINGS HAVE BEEN CREATED THROUGH HIM AND FOR HIM.**
>
> **COLOSSIANS 1:15-16 NASB**

I vote for imitating Jesus.

I n d e x

About the Author

Jim Burns, Ph.D., is President and founder of Homeword. His passion is communicating practical truths to young people and adults to help them live out Christian lives. Highly respected for his expertise in the area of youth ministry, family, and parenting issues, Jim is the author of many books and speaks to thousands of people around the world each year.

Each month in the United States and abroad people either use Jim's written or video materials, hear him speak, or tune in to his radio feature currently airing on over 800 stations and outlets daily. Jim is also a frequent guest on radio programs dealing with parenting issues and youth culture.

He and his wife, Cathy, and their three daughters live in Dana Point, California.

Additional copies of this and other
Honor Books products available
wherever good books are sold.

*Truth Unplugged for Girls: Stories for Girls on
Faith, Love, and Things that Matter Most*

*Truth Unplugged for Guys: Stories for Guys on
Faith, Love, and Things that Matter Most*

If you have enjoyed this book,
or if it has had an impact on your life,
we would like to hear from you.

Please contact us at:

HONOR BOOKS
Cook Communications Ministries, Dept. 201
4050 Lee Vance View
Colorado Springs, CO 80918
Or visit our Web site:
www.cookministries.com

HONOR HB BOOKS

Inspiration and Motivation for the Season of Life